T0243221

Advance Praise for
ROY WHITE: From Compton to the Bronx

"Roy White is as dignified a Yankee as there has ever been, one of the many reasons a generation of fans (myself included) grew up imitating his stance. Paul Semendinger does a masterful job capturing the essence of the great left fielder. This is a must-read about the most underrated Yankee of all time."

Ian O'Connor, four-time New York Times bestselling author of *The Captain: The Journey of Derek Jeter*

"Reading *Roy White: From Compton to the Bronx* is like sitting in a comfortable leather recliner with a cold beverage, listening intently as the Yankee star shares his life story. His rise to stardom was at times a long slog, but determination and moral courage eventually won out. When I put this book down, I knew that what this world needs is more men like Roy White, not just as athletes but as inspirations for future generations."

Alan D. Gaff, author of *Lou Gehrig: The Lost Memoir* and *Field of Corpses*

"In *Roy White: From Compton to the Bronx*, we get the inside story from someone who experienced the highs and lows of being a Yankee like few others. This honest, revealing autobiography tells the story of one of the most underappreciated players in New York baseball history, while adding insight from those who know him best. Whether you remember watching games from the Bronx Zoo era or have only recently come to enjoy the game, this book is a must for any baseball fan."

Chris Donnelly, author of *Doc, Donnie, the Kid, and Billy Brawl: How the 1985 Mets and Yankees Fought For New York's Baseball Soul*

"More than the autobiography of a great player, a revealing portrait of a great man, and a paean to dedication, hard work, and decency."

JB Manheim, author of *The Cooperstown Trilogy*

"The Baseball Gods must have loved watching Roy White play the game of baseball. I really enjoyed reading this book!"

Jonathan A. Fink, author of *The Baseball Gods are Real* and *The Republic Baseball League*

"Roy White traversed a path through the baseball world unlike any other before or since. From Compton to the Bronx is the expertly-told story of his fascinating baseball journey and a portrait of the American dream itself."

Daniel R. Epstein, Co-Director of the Internet Baseball Writers Association of America

"*Roy White: From Compton to the Bronx* reads the way Roy played the game: with class, professionalism and a love for baseball—and no theatrics, braggadocio, scandals or egomania. Kudos to White and Paul Semendinger for telling White's story in a conversational, insightful, fun style. As a Kansas City Royals fan, *Roy White: From Compton to the Bronx* makes me feel kinda bad for rooting so hard against him all those years."

Johnny D. Boggs, author of *Sports on Film: Hollywood History* and the "Baseball Westerns" *Camp Ford*, *The Kansas City Cowboys* and *Buckskin, Bloomers and Me*

"These fascinating stories, rare historic photos and amazing little-known facts about one of the Top 10 Yankees of all-time, Yankee Legend Roy White, will astonish you. *Roy White: From Compton to the Bronx*, an autobiography, is a best-seller in the making. It's the perfect gift for major baseball fans worldwide. Fact: After the 1973 season, karate-do became Roy's secret 'confidence' weapon during off-season training. This page-turner is filled with lots of ah-hah moments and feel-good conversations with Yankee greats such as Joe DiMaggio, Mickey Mantle, Reggie Jackson, Willie Randolph, Goose Gossage, Thurman Munson, and many others. This book is a valuable keepsake and grand-slam homerun!"

Grandmaster Andrew Linick, Publisher: Official Karate Mag., Martial Arts Pioneer, The U.S. Ambassador of Karate™, and International Best-Selling Author: *Nunchaku, Karate's Deadliest Fighting Sticks, 3rd Edition*.

"Yankee fans who grew up in the 1970s love Roy White because of the way he played the game and carried himself. Reading Roy White's story gives fan's an even deeper appreciation for the man behind the Number 6, how he overcame adversities and became a champion--and doing it all with class and humility that make him a true role model. This is a terrific read filled with great memories that truly inspire."

Robert Skead, author of *Something to Prove, the Great Satchel Paige Versus the Rookie Joe DiMaggio*

"Whitey Ford called Roy White 'the most underrated and underappreciated Yankee of all-time.' White could hit, get on base, steal, score a lot of runs and masterfully patrol left field. He is one of the few players to spend 15 seasons with the Yankees. He played in 1,881 games, 7th all-time among Yankees. He also played in three World Series (1976, 1977 and 1978).

Never a flashy or vocal player, White's value to the Yankees was often overlooked. He was quiet, professional and classy. Author Paul Semendinger, and others, make the point that White deserves a spot in Monument Park at Yankee Stadium.

From Compton to the Bronx provides insights into White and his career with the Yankees as a player, coach and executive, as well as his rise through the minors while battling racism and his three-year stint playing for the Yomiuri Giants in Japan.

As a result of this autobiography, White, hopefully, will receive the recognition he deserves."

Barry Sparks, author of *Frank Home Run Baker: Hall of Famer and World Series Hero*

"The Red Sox' succession of left fielders—Ted, Yaz, Rice, Manny—is well-known. But their Yankee counterparts? Not so much. But now, thanks to Paul Semendinger, we get the autobiography of Roy White, the gentlemanly All-Star who for years graced the vast acreage of Yankee Stadium's outfield. There may be a lot to learn about this overlooked position in Yankee history, but *Roy White: From Compton to the Bronx* is a damn good place to start."

David Ostrowsky, Atlanta Jewish Times

ROY WHITE:
From Compton to the Bronx

By
Roy White

with Paul Semendinger

Artemesia
Publishing

ISBN: 978-1-951122-57-7 (cloth)
ISBN: 978-1-951122-32-4 (ebook)
LCCN: 2022949297
Artemesia Publishing
9 Mockingbird Hill Rd
Tijeras, New Mexico 87059
www.apbooks.net
info@artemesiapublishing.com

Table of Contents

Foreword by Marty Appel..1

Introduction..5

Prologue: My Greatest Baseball Memory........................9

Chapter 1: From Compton… 13

Chapter 2: The Start of My Professional Baseball Journey....23

Playing with Roy White in the Minor Leagues
by Ian Dixon..39

Chapter 3: ...To The Bronx...45

Chapter 4: My Early Years in the Big Leagues.............51

Chapter 5: Putting It All Together....................................63

Chapter 6: The Final CBS Years.......................................77

Chapter 7: The First Years with George Steinbrenner....87

Photos: 109

Playing on the Yankees with Roy White
by Chris Chambliss...125

Chapter 8: The First World Series...................................129

Chapter 9: World Series Champions...............................139

Chapter 10: World Series Champions Again.................149

Playing and Coaching for the Yankees with Roy White
by Willie Randolph...159

Chapter 11: My Last Season in the Major Leagues.................163

Chapter 12: Playing for the Yomiuri Giants.................169

Playing Baseball in Japan with Roy White
by John Sipin...183

Chapter 13: Now a Coach..189

Chapter 14: The Front Office..195

What Roy White Means to the Yankees
by Ray Negron..199

Chapter 15: In and Out of Baseball...............................205

Collaborating on the Roy White Foundation
by Murray Bauer...215

Chapter 16: The Former Ball Player..221
Appendix 1..227
Appendix 2..233
Appendix 3..239
Appendix 4..241
Appendix 5..243
Appendix 6..245
Appendix 7..247
About the Authors...249

Acknowledgements

Roy White: There are so many people to thank, beginning with my parents. I am appreciative of the fact that my mom let me play baseball as much as I wanted to as a kid. I appreciate Johnny Keane for giving me my first shot as a big leaguer and for Ralph Houk sticking with me when I initially struggled and for making me a fulltime outfielder. I am thankful for all my great teammates and friends in the game. Of course, I also wish to acknowledge and thank my wife Linda and my great children Loreena and Reade.

Paul Semendinger: This book would never have been possible without Roy White believing in me. I'll never be able to thank him enough for that. Likewise, I wouldn't be a respected published author without the support and encouragement of Geoff Habiger of Artemesia Publishing. Thank you, Geoff, for also believing in me.

Thank you to the many people who offered advice, suggestions, and helped with proofing the manuscript. This includes Mike Whiteman, Jack Hirsch, Dave Connolly, and each of my sons, Ryan, Alex, and Ethan. And to Richard Cuicchi for his tremendously detailed final edit of this work. My parents also played, as they always do, a huge supporting role in all of this.

Thank you to Dr. Brian Chinni for helping me revitalize the Roy White Foundation with its first public event in many years and for his proof of this manuscript as well.

Thank you, of course, to my wonderful wife Laurie who encourages me and loves me even when I talk baseball incessantly and seem to care more about ballplayers than fixing or doing things around the house.

Thank you, of course, to God and Jesus without whom none of this would be possible.

Foreword
By Marty Appel

Marty Appel, a Yankee historian and former public relations official with the team, is the author of Pinstripe Empire, Munson, and Casey Stengel.

***

PUBLIC RELATIONS OFFICIALS AT Major League teams, of which I was one, tend to deal with the biographical material you find on the backs of baseball cards. Date of birth, place of birth, height, weight, bats, throws, and the traditional baseball card stats we have long been familiar with.

The birth of Baseball-Reference.com has increased our knowledge by adding schooling, draft information and other baseball necessities.

When Roy White joined the Yankees, we took care of business and handled the need-to-know items.

We didn't look forward—to his becoming the greatest left fielder in the history of the New York Yankees—and we didn't look backwards. We didn't ask, "Are you the product of an interracial marriage? Were your parents divorced? Was your family on welfare? Was your mother an alcoholic? Was your father absent for your childhood? Did you grow up in a tough neighborhood? Did you have street fights? Did you ever spend time in jail? Were you ever beaten up? Did you carry a weapon?"

Those weren't subjects likely to be covered in the Yankees Yearbook.

Even if those questions were appropriate—and they

weren't—you wouldn't go there while having a conversation with Roy. He was quiet, unassuming, classy, professional, serious, and dignified. I remember that he would lug a record player on road trips (long before MP3), where he would room with Horace Clarke and play jazz in the room. It was hardly an activity that made one wonder where this guy grew up!

When I was writing about him once, long after we had both moved on, I learned that he was a member of street gang. It seemed so out of place.

"What were you, the recording secretary?" I asked. "You kept the minutes?"

I'm sure Roy was not the only Major League player who, when you peeled back the onion, you found there so much more to learn. Even if I had that knowledge, and could have tipped off a writer to ask about those things, it still would have felt like an invasion of his privacy.

And truth be told, many, many players had lives that were less than Little League to the Majors with the Cleaver family waiting at home with dinner.

The fact was, everyone liked Roy White. There wasn't a more likeable member of the team. He and his beautiful wife Linda were guests at my 1975 wedding. I loved that they made the long trip. When our son was born, we visited their New Jersey home and enjoyed the day with their kids.

As the years moved on and he stayed with the team, appreciation rose. He was on his way to becoming a very senior member of this storied franchise, one who broke in while Mickey Mantle, Whitey Ford and Roger Maris were on the team, and one who stayed to be teammates with Thurman Munson, Reggie Jackson, Catfish Hunter and Willie Randolph. Of all the inspiring stories that arose from those Yankee teams of the late '70s, Roy hitting a big home run in the 1978 ALCS warmed the hearts of everyone who had been there through the tough years of 1965-75. He got to see the promised land.

How many others would spend at least 15 seasons in the Major Leagues, all with the Yankees? By the end of Roy's playing career there were only five others—Lou Gehrig, Bill Dickey, Frank Crosetti, Mickey Mantle, and Whitey Ford.

(Later Derek Jeter, Jorge Posada, Mariano Rivera, and Bernie Williams joined this small club.)

The question of naming a team's "all-time team" gets sidetracked on the Yankees by having Ruth, DiMaggio and Mantle as the outfielders, disregarding the left-center-right matter. Of the three, only Ruth played some left field, depending on the sun. Usually, he was in right. But if the question is specifically tied to that difficult acreage known as "death valley"—left field of Yankee Stadium—to me, Roy emerges on top. Others who would be in the discussion would be Bob Meusel, Charlie Keller, Dave Winfield and Hideki Matsui, but none had Roy's longevity, or indeed, consistency playing just that outfield position. He mastered it. He played a full season errorlessly out there. He dealt with the sun field that was left field in Yankee Stadium, and he led all left fielders in assists twice, in fielding percentage five times, and in putouts eight times. As sportswriter Bryan Hoch points out, among Yankee left fielders he is first in plate appearances, at bats, runs, hits and walks, while placing second in doubles, home runs, RBIs and stolen bases.

The home runs always seem to catch us by surprise, because he was not a big muscle-bound slugger but a lithe, fast-footed athlete who often choked up at the plate. (*SPORT* magazine once ran a story titled "The Yankees have a Clean Up Hitter Who Chokes Up.") And before the proliferation of switch hitters in the game's current era, he was among the all-time switch-hitting leaders in home runs. And in homering from both sides of the plate in the same game, on the Yankees there was Mantle (10 times), and White (five times). Posada (7), Mark Teixeira (7) Williams (6) and Nick Swisher (5) are a part of the current long ball era.

He even set a single-season American League sacrifice fly record of 17 in 1971, which has lasted more than half a century without being surpassed. We gave him a plaque for that one, thinking there are no such plaques generally presented. That is clutch hitting.

For a PR guy like myself, Roy was a dream. Did we need someone to shake hands and pose for pictures with some sponsors on the field, which required him to get dressed in full uniform long before he needed to? Roy was our go-to guy. Did we need someone to record some promos for our out-of-town radio network? Roy would bring that late-night deep disk jockey voice to the microphone, and it was like we were dealing with James Earl Jones or Morgan Freeman.

Were there pre-game autographs to sign for kids by the railing? There was a good chance Roy was among those answering the call.

When he went to Japan at the end of his Major League career, he had a chance to be a teammate of the legendary Sadaharu Oh, as he had been to Mickey Mantle. No one else could make that claim, and I could see Roy's inner Zen guiding him through his time there. I imagine his respect for the game as well as his respect for teammates made him much admired, and he won a Japanese World Series as he had won our World Series, (twice,) also a unique accomplishment.

When people talk about those two Yankee seals of approval, the plaque in Monument Park and the retired number, I nod in agreement. As for retiring his number, the Yankees did retire number six for Joe Torre—even though he usually wore a jacket, and few could tell you what his number was! It feels like it could have been retired for both, as "8" is for Berra and Dickey. The plaque? Well, his time may come. We hope it does.

Introduction
By Paul Semendinger, Ed.D.

I **ALWAYS WANTED TO** be a New York Yankee. I'm in my mid-fifties now, still pitching in two baseball leagues, and still hoping the Yankees decide to take a chance on me. Baseball is in my blood and has been since I was eight years old watching the Yankees on television and falling in love with the game, the players, the stories, and so much more.

The 1977 Yankees players are all legends to me. Superheroes. They are all larger than life. I grew up watching Reggie Jackson, Willie Randolph, Thurman Munson, Ron Guidry, Graig Nettles, Chris Chambliss, Bucky Dent, Sparky Lyle, Mickey Rivers, Lou Piniella, Roy White, and so many others. They were my heroes. They were superheroes. Still are.

All I knew about baseball back then was that it was a wonderful game, that the Yankees were great, and that they always won the World Series. I loved them all. My favorite player was Graig Nettles. It might have been Roy White, but he was already taken.

In 1977, the coolest person on TV was Fonzie. I grew up across the street from two teenage twin boys who were both as cool to me as The Fonz. The Twins (as I knew them) were Yankees fans. Their favorite player was Roy White. They idolized him. As such, I did as well. But I guess they talked about baseball with my sister first. She was older than me and she claimed Roy White as her own. By the logic of childhood, I couldn't have the same favorite player as my older sister. Still, Roy White stood atop that pedestal reserved for our childhood heroes. He couldn't be my favorite, but he was still a favorite. Roy White stood on that pedestal of greatness. This is where we put the heroes of our youth. It's where Roy White resides today. And where he'll reside always and forever in my memories and in my heart.

We don't usually get the chance to meet our heroes. Often, if we do, we find they aren't like we hoped. Somehow our heroes fall short in so many ways. Many do. Maybe most. But not all. Some heroes turn out to be better people than we would have thought. Roy White turned out to be a better human being than I could have ever hoped or imagined.

***

It was late in 2021. I was still an elementary school principal at the time, working through my final year before retirement. I had written a few books. I had won a few writing awards. I ran a successful Yankees blog and was a frequent contributor on some baseball and sports podcasts. But in the world of writing and big media and all of that, I was a nobody.

My friend John "Mac" McGrath introduced me to Roy, sort of. He had interviewed Roy White for a podcast on the North East Streaming Sports Network. I was unable to participate, but I asked Mac to speak to Roy and to let him know that I would be happy to write his autobiography. I, and so many others, have always felt that Roy White's story needed to be told. Mac did just that, and the next thing I knew, he sent me Roy White's phone number.

One thing led to the next, we texted back and forth, and then Roy actually called me one day as I was driving home from work. After quickly recovering from shock, I pulled off on a side street and I told him of my hopes to write his story. Amazingly, a few days later, after thinking it over, he agreed. The next thing I knew, we were talking regularly on the phone and meeting at our favorite location, Panera Bread, to talk about his career, the Yankees, and more. Roy White and I met often. He'd talk. I'd ask questions and type as quickly as I could. Within seven or eight months, the initial draft of this manuscript was completed.

Every single time we met, Roy White was kind and humble and patient and accommodating. I never wanted to be a fan, I always wanted to be just me, the writer. I never wore a Yankees shirt or hat, although sometimes Roy White did. As we talked, we'd laugh. He'd tell great stories about my childhood heroes (and his heroes as well) and as he did, I just kept trying to get it all down and not miss a thing.

Who is Roy White as a person? I have a few stories that I believe illustrate who he is. First, he trusted me, and I'm not sure why, to write his story. This is a great honor for me. I had never before been befriended by a Major League Baseball player. And this was no ordinary player – this was a Yankees legend and a childhood hero. This was Roy White. Sometimes legends only associate with legends. It's rare that one gives an unknown a shot at something great. But Roy White did.

Even today, Roy White is extremely popular. The cheers for him at Old Timer's Day at Yankee Stadium often ring the loudest. When people recognize him, they go out of their way to tell him how much he means to their lives – even today and even from afar. Roy White's phone rings often – from all sorts of people who seek a story or a quote, or from old teammates and friends. Roy White remains extremely busy, yet, out of blue on Father's Day I received a text from him wishing me a great day. This famous ballplayer took time from his day to remember me. That's class.

As I stated, when we met, I tried to never be a fan. I was always the writer. I never asked for a photo together. I never asked for an autograph for myself. I did, though, ask for one favor. One of the twins from my childhood came down with colon cancer. I broke my own rule and asked Roy White to sign a card for him. Roy did this gladly. (When I gave the card to my old neighbor, his eyes filled with tears. It was that meaningful to him.)

In July 2022, I was interviewed about my Yankees book, *The Least Among Them,* on Pat Williams' radio program. As we talked, he told me the following story:

Pat Williams began his professional sports career as a minor league baseball player. In his first game as a professional, his team was playing against the Ft. Lauderdale Yankees. This was a game in the lowest level of the minor leagues. In Williams' first at bat, he struck out on three pitches. In his second at bat, he struck out on three pitches again. Things certainly were not going well for him. In his third at bat, he found himself down with no balls and two strikes. He was one pitch away from striking out for the third time, on only nine total pitches. He then swung at the next offering and connected and went to second base with a double. The second baseman on that Yankees team came over to congratulate him and welcome him to pro baseball. That player, the one who first made Pat Williams feel like a pro, the one who gave him some of his first words of encouragement, was Roy White. That's who Roy White was. And it is who he still is today.

I have talked to a host of people about Roy White, some of whom are quoted in this book—former players, executives, coaches, and fans. The same words are said over and over. I'm told about what a kind and decent human being Roy White is. I'm told what a gentleman he is. I'm told about what a great baseball player he was—and what he meant to the Yankees and the fans. He was the single player who covered the era between the great Yankees teams of the 1960s and the World Championship Yankees of the late 1970s. Roy White was the only player to play for the Yankees for the entire decade of the 1970s. He is a Yankees legend. (And I believe it is unconscionable that he has not been recognized with a plaque in Monument Park in Yankee Stadium.)

But the word that people use most often when talking about Roy White is "class."

That word defines him perfectly. Roy White is class. Roy White is, simply, a quiet, dignified, exceptional human being. That's class. That's Roy White—a true gentleman, a legend of the game, a Yankee. He was a Yankees legend, but he is an even better person.

This is his story. This is the story of Roy White.

I am honored that I had the opportunity to write this with him.

Prologue
My Greatest Baseball Memory

I HAD AN EXTREMELY memorable baseball career full of many great moments. There were so many highlights that I sometimes find it difficult to recount them all, but when I stop to think about it, they all come back, slowly, one by one. I have been blessed to have lived the life that I have. Baseball, of course, has been a big part of who I was and who I still am.

People often ask me to recount my greatest baseball memory. Some who remember me ask me about specific moments. I'll list a few here, all of which were great and are dear memories, but none of which ranks as my greatest memory.

- In my first Major League game, I singled in my first at bat (off Dave McNally of the Orioles). I later scored on a base hit by Tom Tresh. That was in 1965.
- I became known as an outfielder, but I played second base in my first big league starting assignment, a game in which I had two hits.
- The next year (1966), I hit my first big league homer off Sam McDowell (who would one day be my teammate).
- I batted fourth, behind the great Mickey Mantle. I was there to protect him in the batting order.
- I was a two-time American League All-Star.
- I once went an entire season (1971) without making an error in the field. I was the first Yankee to do that!
- I played in the World Series in 1976, 1977, and 1978. We won the World Series, of course, in 1977 and 1978.
- I had some big post season hits including the game winning home run to win the American League

Championship Series in 1978 and another home run in the 1978 World Series.

- It was my bat that Bucky Dent used to hit his famous home run in Boston (also in 1978).
- In Japan, I got to play alongside the great Sadaharu Oh. Once again, I hit fourth in the batting order to protect Japan's greatest home run hitter.
- I am one of only two players in baseball history to play for a winning team in the World Series and the Japan Series (which we won in 1981).
- I served as a Major League Coach and as a front office executive.
- I helped found the Roy White Foundation to assist high school graduates with some of the costs associated with attending college
- Even today, more than forty years after my last Major League baseball game, fans approach me and tell me that they loved the way I played the game.

I'll tell those stories and many more over the pages of this book. This is my story, the story of my life and my baseball journey. I am glad to have the chance to share it with you.

As for my greatest baseball memory, well, it was something a bit simpler than just hitting a home run, making a catch, or being part of something memorable. My greatest baseball memory was when I walked into the Yankees clubhouse in Yankee Stadium in 1965 as a player for the very first time. I walked in and looked around the room. I saw Mickey Mantle, Whitey Ford, Elston Howard and Roger Maris. When I was a kid in Little League, I was watching these players. I had their baseball cards. And now, here I was, one of them. I was a big leaguer. I was a New York Yankee.

I remember Tom Tresh, who had been the American League Rookie of the Year in 1962, coming over to me and stating that he was glad that I was part of the team. Phil Linz and then other players did so too.

These weren't just any baseball players; these were the New York Yankees. The great New York Yankees. These

Yankees had been to the World Series the previous year, and the year before that, and the year before that too. These were the Yankees that had been to the World Series 14 times in the previous 16 years. This wasn't just a great team... these players were part of the greatest dynasty of all time.

And there I was, now part of it. I was welcomed by these players into their locker room as an equal member of this distinguished squad. I soon got to know all of these players personally. I was a New York Yankee.

What could be greater than that?

Chapter 1
From Compton...
1943-1961

IT TAKES A LOT of hard work to make it to the Major Leagues. It takes even more work to be an All-Star, and a World Champion, and to play in the big leagues for fifteen seasons, but it all has to start somewhere. My start came on the streets in Los Angeles and Compton. It wasn't an easy beginning.

I was born in Los Angeles, California on December 27, 1943, into a mixed-race family. My father, Marcus White, was of German, Austrian, and Czech descent. He was an artist and would become a well-known one at that. My mother, Margaret, was African American. As I look back on my parents' marriage, I realize that this couldn't have been easy for them. Mixed-race families were not common in the 1940s. In fact, possibly in order to allow them to get married, my father listed his race on the marriage certificate as negro. My parents were decades, if not a century (in many regards), ahead of their time. As I said, this could not have been easy on them, and it wasn't. Because of the societal pressures they faced, they were not able to make the marriage last.

A few years before my parents divorced, I had a big health scare. I contracted polio. This was when I was six or seven years old. I was fortunate in that my grandmother was a nurse's aide, so she knew the signs of this terrible disease. It all started innocently enough. I came home from school complaining of a fever and a headache along with a good deal of fatigue. My grandmother immediately recognized these troubling signs and called an ambulance. The next thing I knew, I was in the hospital where I would stay for the next few months. The doctors and the nurses gave me daily injections of penicillin to help me recover. I missed so much school that when I returned, they put me back a grade. Fortunately, I was able to catch back up and they returned me to second grade where I belonged. I was also very fortunate in that I had no lasting effects from the polio.

Once my parents were divorced, we moved around a lot. My mom was on welfare—public assistance. It was tough for her to make ends meet as my mom was an alcoholic. By the time I was eight or nine-years-old, we'd settled in Compton on 131st Street. This is where I really started to play ball. We didn't have a lot of money; public assistance did what it could and my mom worked a bit by raising German Shepherds. There were always a few dogs in the house. I remember that she was able to sell the puppies for $30 each. It was never easy, though. But she loved us and supported us as best as she could.

I never grew up with us having much money. In fact, oftentimes we had little to none. I remember being home when the bill collectors from the county would come and we couldn't answer the door because they'd be asking us to pay bills that we couldn't pay. The same was true of the electric company. There were weeks when we were without lights because my mom didn't have enough money to pay the bills.

Each year for school, I was given just a few pairs of pants and a couple of shirts. If I needed a new pair of pants, and I didn't do this often, I'd shoplift them. There wasn't another way. I did this out of necessity. Thank God, I never got caught. I had just one pair of shoes. Those shoes also had to last all year. Some years, I'd have to tape my shoes to keep them together.

We never had a lot to eat as well. For lunch, when I brought lunch to school (sometimes I'd get lunch in the cafeteria), I often had a mayonnaise sandwich—just mayo and bread. The other staple I had was bologna and cheese. By the time I was in high school, I worked in the school's cafeteria. Those years I would always have a lunch to eat. The one day of the year when we would have food was Thanksgiving. I always looked forward to the turkey and all the trimmings. This wasn't just a special day on the calendar for us to eat a lot, it was the only day we could eat a lot.

My mom didn't make any of us kids work. My sister Sonja was a few years older than me, and I had a little brother, Bruce, who was also naturally athletic. Even though things weren't easy, my mom encouraged us all to be athletic. We all took dance lessons at one point or another. My mom also let me play as much as I wanted. And I played a lot of baseball, a lot of baseball in various forms.

In addition to playing, as I was growing up, I also watched a lot of baseball. We'd watch the games from the Pacific Coast League on TV. I remember seeing games from the old Wrigley Field and Gilmore Stadium in Los Angeles. We rooted for the Los Angeles Angels and the Hollywood Stars. Some of the players we watched made the Major Leagues. I remember Steve Bilko, a huge home run hitter. And Dick Stuart. There were so many great players, Leon Wagner, Ed Bailey, Bill Mazeroski, Jim Brosnan, and Ryne Duren. Future managers Gene Mauch and George Bamberger also played in that league as I was growing up.

Like all the kids, I collected baseball cards, but we didn't save them. We did as all the kids did, we'd look at them, trade them, and put them into our tires to make our bicycles sound like motorcycles.

I was a fan of the Cincinnati Reds mostly. I loved their uniforms with the cut sleeves. They were the originals with sleeveless uniforms, which I thought was really cool. They had some big stars, big hitters, guys like Ted Kluszewski who was just so strong. I think they started with the cut sleeves to allow Kluszewski to show off his huge muscles. There were other great players as well—Wally Post, Gus Bell, Frank Robinson, Ed Bailey. I remember Johnny Temple and Roy McMillan as a great double play combination. Those Reds always seemed to be in the pennant race, but they never had quite enough pitching. Later, when I was a Yankees coach in the 1980s, those teams faced a similar problem. Those were teams with great hitters, terrific players, but just not quite enough pitching to get them to the top of the standings.

I also rooted a bit for the Cleveland Indians. They also had the nice flashy uniforms. I rooted for the Indians over the New York Giants in the 1954 World Series. I remember coming home from school for lunch in 1954 and seeing Willie Mays make his famous catch on TV robbing Vic Wertz of a big hit. I saw the catch and then I had to go back to school. I was heartbroken when the Indians lost, because they were supposed to win that series easily. They had Bob Lemon and Early Wynn and Mike Garcia, all great pitchers, who, along with Bob Feller, were known as the Big Four. Ray Narleski too. They also had some great players like Larry Doby and Vic Wertz. That 1954 Indians team was the only non-Yankees team to make it to the World Series in the years from 1949 through 1958. In those days, the Yankees totally dominated baseball.

When I was in high school, to help get some spending money, I worked in a place that rented washing machines. There was a Post Office next door, and they had a dumpster out back where they'd throw away stuff that they couldn't mail. I'd sometimes look through the paper garbage and find old *SPORT* magazines with guys like Ted Williams and Stan "The Man" Musial on the covers and read the articles and dream of being a big leaguer myself.

But my path to the Major Leagues was in no way straight forward. On my first Little League team, they put me in right field. That's where you put the worst player. I didn't know how to catch the ball the right way. I didn't know how to hold my glove upwards to catch it. I'd try to catch everything in a basket, like Willie Mays. I had to learn a lot. On those teams, early on, when I was nine or ten, we didn't get uniforms, we just got a T-shirt and a cap. I was a long way away from Yankees pinstripes.

I practiced a lot, and slowly got better. We were able to play baseball year-round because of the warm weather. We formed our own league among the kids in the neighborhood. We couldn't afford a baseball so we would take an old sock and stuff it with other socks or rags or soft stuff and tie it up like a baseball. We'd pitch from 30 feet away and we could make that ball do amazing things. We could throw curves and sliders and more. For us kids, this was a highly competitive way to play. We called this the "Sock Ball League."

My backyard usually became the Polo Grounds or Crosley Field. We knew all the big league ballparks. Forbes Field. Ebbets Field. Each week we'd have our own "Game of the Week" sort of a take-off of the weekly baseball games shown on NBC-TV. Some of my best friends were the kids from the Neal family who lived behind us. They played a lot of baseball with me. We had all sorts of rules for what happened depending on where you hit the ball. If it hit in one spot, it was a single, another place was a home run. We also had to bat like the players on the team that was playing. If Stan Musial was batting, I'd have to hit left-handed. Duke Snider too. We imitated all the different players when we'd play. This was how I learned to switch-hit. I also hit a lot when I was alone. We had lots of stones in our driveway. I would hit them into our backyard pretending to be the various players. I'd be Pee Wee Reese, Jim Gilliam, Duke Snider, all the Dodgers, or whatever team I was emulating. Sometimes I would even get Roy White into those imaginary Dodgers lineups. When I'd bat, I'd always try to hit a home run. Pee Wee Reese hit singles with those stones. I hit homers.

As I grew up, there were a bunch of great players who I played with or against in those years, many who became Major Leaguers. This list includes Reggie Smith (who played for the Red Sox, Cardinals, and Dodgers), Don Wilson (who pitched for the Astros), Dave Nelson (Indians), and Lenny Randle (who played for the Rangers and the Mets). We all played on the sandlots, in Little League, and in Connie Mack ball, and in the American Legion leagues, as well as in high school.

One very good ballplayer from our neighborhood was Dave Kelly. He was a local star. There was no doubt that he was the best player in the neighborhood. Eventually, he got $50,000 to sign with the Detroit Tigers. He reached Double-A. I played against him in the minor leagues. Making it all the way to the big leagues, though, is tough. As great as he was as a kid, he never made it.

As I played, I got better, of course, and was moved from the outfield and became an infielder. At Centennial High School, I moved to second base which allowed Dave Kelly to play shortstop. A few years later, Reggie Smith joined the team and played third base. We were one of the best programs in the state and were big rivals with Compton High.

By this time, seeing the players around me signing contracts, I knew that I would also play professionally. There was a lot of talent that surrounded me. Of note, these were in the years before there was an amateur baseball draft. Scouts would come to our games and our homes and offer us contracts. I was holding my own and was able to compete with the best of the ballplayers on the sandlots, the school teams, and on the semi-pro teams. I just knew the scouts would be coming to my home eventually as well.

One of the best players at our rival Compton High was Ronnie Woods. In my senior year, I hit .475. That was very good, but Ronnie batted .620! He was always getting hits, two or three a game. And when he batted, the way he stood, it looked like he'd hit every ball right at me at second base, even though he was a right-handed batter. He had quick, fast wrists, just like Hank Aaron, and he'd smash the ball down the third base line. Ronnie signed for $25,000 with the Pirates. We eventually played together with the Yankees for a few years (from 1969 to 1971). Unfortunately, Ronnie got beaned in the minor leagues and was never the hitter he could have been. Things like that change a player. The same thing happened to Paul Blair of the Baltimore Orioles and who was later my teammate on the Yankees. Ronnie Woods had great talent and he could have been a huge star. I know this, there was no one better than him in Southern California when we played.

Some of the stars at the other schools at the time included Jim Rooker who pitched for the Pirates, Paul Schaal, who played for the Royals, and the Lefebvre brothers. Jim Lefebvre ended up playing for the Dodgers. I truly grew up in a hotbed of baseball.

But life was not always easy. The streets of Compton were not safe. The most dangerous part of Los Angeles at the time was Watts which was just a couple of blocks away from where I lived. There were times when I came very close to getting badly hurt, or worse.

I remember when I was twelve- or thirteen-years old walking with my sister Sonja and her friend at night. We were walking my sister's friend home a few blocks into Watts. Out of the dark, four people jumped us. I got pulled down to the sidewalk, but I was able to get up and run. I was lucky. Sonja too. She also escaped. But my sister's friend was beaten up badly. She suffered broken ribs and a concussion and was in the hospital for a month.

Another time, a few years later, by this time I was in high school, I was with the Neal brothers and our friend Rudy Darlington. Rudy also played ball. He was a right-handed pitcher, and was pretty good, but he also had a bit of thug in him which prevented him from being as good as he could have been. One day, as we went past the Little League field, a car pulled up with four or five guys in it. They asked if we wanted to fight. We all just kept walking, but Rudy started to engage them. Soon we heard guys behind us with chains and tire irons. Again, we knew we better start running!

As I ran, I saw the Little League field and ran through the open fence in that direction. As I ran across the outfield, the grass was wet, and I slipped and fell. I figured I was about to get beaten. I laid in the grass in left field waiting... and nothing happened. They must not have seen me duck into the field, so no one followed. I then got up and ran like hell to get home. Years later, when I was in left field in Yankee Stadium, I thought of that moment—almost getting killed in left field at the Little League park when I was a high school kid. I had come a long way.

When I was sixteen years old, I worked in a liquor store doing stock work and making deliveries. I'd take the bottles and ride with them on my bike into all different parts of the city, even Watts. I'd deliver the bottles, get paid in cash, and then pedal back to the store. I was a sitting duck to get hit or to have someone steal the alcohol or money, or both, but somehow, in that job, no one bothered me.

I wasn't always a well-behaved kid. One summer, when we were in junior high, Rudy and I, and a few other kids, did some misbehaving. We broke into some school cafeterias and stole ice cream. In order to get into the schools, we would break some windows. We didn't have a lot of money, and the ice cream was a good treat. But that was Rudy, too. He was an instigator. Interestingly, we never got caught, or at least not initially.

A few years later, I was called out of a high school class to go to the principal's office where a police officer was waiting for me. He took me to the station, and they questioned me about what I had done those few years previous. I was part of the Great Ice Cream Robberies. By then I had gone straight, and I admitted it all. My friends had only admitted to breaking into a school or two. I confessed to all of them—maybe four schools in total. After my admission, the police locked me in a cell for a few hours and my mom had to come get me.

Then, in Juvenile Court, they reviewed my record. I was very frightened about being sent to Juvenile Detention. Rudy was sent there. It wasn't good. But, by then, I had good grades in school, all A's and B's in college prep classes too, so they gave me probation. That fortunate decision helped change my life.

Not everyone from the neighborhood found success. Rudy died years later from drugs.

By my senior year in high school, I was also playing football. My friend Arthur Tolliver told me to go out for the team. We played football in the streets, and he knew I was quick. I was only 150 pounds, and I didn't like the idea of being tackled by the big guys, but it was great fun.

On my first ever play in high school football, I took the ball on a kickoff and ran it back for a touchdown. I guess my speed really paid off.

On offense, I played as a back, running with the ball or blocking for the quarterback. The competition was tough, though. I played against Roy Jefferson who later was an All-Pro with the Pittsburgh Steelers. I also played against Jack Snow, another future NFL All-Pro. Think about that, I had to block those guys! (Most of the time they ran right through me.) I was fortunate that we had Larry Todd as our quarterback. He could scramble. He later played for the Oakland Raiders. It's amazing how much athletic talent was in Compton and the surrounding areas at the time.

By the end of my senior year in high school, I had scholarship offers from UCLA to play baseball and from Long Beach State University to play football. But I knew if I received an offer to play professional baseball, then that's what I would do. I actually expected to get a big offer. Bob Bailey, who played at Long Beach at Woodrow Wilson High School, had recently signed for $100,000 with the Pirates. The neighborhood boys were all hot commodities. I figured, since I played as well as them, that I'd be one too.

But life doesn't always go as we plan or wish. No offers came for me. Initially I was puzzled. I knew I had the talent. I had offers from UCLA and Long Beach State, so I knew if I wasn't going to play ball, I had options. I later learned that there were a few teams that might have been interested in me, including the Los Angeles Angels, but they thought I was going to college. In June, long after the other players in my neighborhood and against whom I played had signed contracts, a Yankees scout, Tuffy Hashem, eventually arrived at my door. He met with me personally, my mom didn't get involved in this discussion, and said that the Yankees would like to sign me. He said, "You're our type of ballplayer." This was the last thing I expected. The Yankees had been the furthest thing from my mind. And there was no indication that the Yankees were interested in me. We all knew who the scouts were and when they were watching us. When Tuffy stated that he'd been watching me for a while, I was very surprised. I'd never seen him before!

Hashem told me that the Yankees would offer me all of $6,000. He also said he'd give me a few days to think it over. I didn't know what to do. $6,000 was still a lot of money, but it wasn't anything like what the other guys had been signing for. To be honest, based on the bonuses the other guys were getting, this seemed very low to me. But, still, it was an offer. And it came from the New York Yankees. Without a dad at home, I consulted with my high school coach David Carlyle and my American Legion coach, a man we called "Hot Rod." He said, "Roy, this is what you always wanted. This is your opportunity." And, of course, this was with the Yankees. The great New York Yankees who were always in the World Series. I agreed and took his advice.

I signed the contract soon after. I was paid $1,000 on approval of the contract, and then would get $2,000, the next year, on July 1, 1962, $2,000 on July 1, 1963, and $1,000 on July 1, 1964. I would also receive a bonus of $4,000 on "assignment of contract to a major league club." That would be my goal. It was my goal, my dream, and my hope.

But first I had to prove I deserved it.

My trek into and through the minor leagues was about to begin._

Chapter 2
The Start of My Professional Baseball Journey
1962-1964

I **WAS NOW A** professional baseball player, so of course, I spent the summer playing American Legion and summer ball at home. Tuffy Hashem had said that I wasn't going to report to the minor leagues that year because I had signed so late. I signed the contract on July 1 which was halfway through the minor league season. Most of the other guys had signed months before. With the late start, Tuffy Hashem didn't feel that I'd get an even start, so I was a professional ballplayer playing unprofessionally at home for one more summer.

There were a number of future big leaguers who I played with that summer in various leagues and for various teams. Chet Brewer, a great former pitcher who played in the Negro Leagues ran a baseball program in Watts, California and he would gather up some of the best talent for the games. I played for Chet as did Willie Crawford, who later played for the Dodgers, Bobby Tolan, a future member of the Reds and Phillies, and Dock Ellis, who pitched for the Pirates and would one day be my teammate on the Yankees.

That summer I purchased a car with some of my money from the Yankees. The car, as I recall, was $500 which ate up a lot of my initial cash, but I needed to get around to play baseball. My friend "Wally" Jones, also a ballplayer, got me a job that summer building the trailers for tractor trailer trucks. We'd spend hours each day using rivets to put the side panels on the trucks. It was hard and exhausting work. In southern California, in the summer, it was always hot. I needed the money, so I did it, but I much preferred playing baseball to that type of manual labor.

I later found out that the Yankees, even though they signed me, didn't even know who I was. Tuffy Hashem had signed six guys (including me) that year without the Yankees' permission. I was the only one of the six players to eventually reach the big leagues. Hashem never even sent the Yankees a scouting report on me. He just signed me and the other guys. That's probably why my deal was for such little money. Not long after he signed us, he no longer worked for the Yankees. Amazing. I didn't learn about this until years later when Johnny Johnson, a Yankee farm director, told me that story. Later, Joe Trimble of the New York Daily News wrote this in a newspaper article, also after I had reached the Yankees. It is almost unbelievable. The guy who signed me did so without permission from the big club. I might have been the Yankees' "type of ballplayer," but the Yankees didn't even know who I was.

That fall, I enrolled at Compton Junior College. I was an art major. Art must run in my family. My sister would become a professional dancer. I would even end up as an art dealer after my playing days. And my dad would become a well-known artist himself. But that was all in the future; at that point he was just driving a cab in Los Angeles. We were all still starting to find our ways.

As the year turned to 1962, I remember waiting in anxious and eager anticipation for my letter from the Yankees to report to Spring Training. I figured the letter would come in January. It didn't. I look back today and am glad I didn't know that I was signed without permission from the Yankees. Had I known that at the time I might have figured they weren't going to invite me to Spring Training and that my career was over before it even began. But, in February, the letter, containing the reporting instructions, finally arrived. I was on my way. My trip into professional baseball would begin with a flight, the first time I would ever be in an airplane. I was to fly out of Los Angeles to Tampa, Florida.

After landing, the next part of the journey involved a bus ride to Haines City where the Yankees had their complex for their players in the lowest levels of the minor leagues. The Class D, Class C, and Class B players all trained at Haines City. The Single-A, Double-A, and Triple-A teams trained in Bartow, Florida.

A whole series of new experiences awaited me in Florida, and not all of these were good. Segregation was real and very much alive in 1962. I had never before been judged or treated differently because of the color of my skin. That was about to change quickly.

For that first Spring Training, I stayed at the Haines City Hotel. There was a daily routine that we followed. We'd have breakfast at the hotel and then be shuttled in cars to the baseball complex. At the complex, we'd get our uniforms for the day. These were old hand-me-down Yankees uniforms. One day you might get Moose Skowron's pants, the next day you might be wearing Tony Kubek's. Needless to say, these uniforms didn't fit well, and we didn't look too sharp, but this was how it was done. We didn't get a chance to think about much. We did as we were told and just went out and played the game as best as we were able.

It was a great experience, playing ball as a new professional. I got to meet guys from all over the United States. These were great players, most of them white, like the guys at the hotel with me, but there were several other black players as well.

One day, at lunch, Leroy Reams, an 18-year-old rookie like myself, a black guy from Oakland, California said, "Roy, I see you here playing ball every day, but I never see you at night. Where are you staying?" I told him that I was at the Haines City Hotel. He replied, "You can't stay there." The Haines City Hotel was segregated and reserved for whites only. I guess because of my lighter skin complexion; they must have assumed I was a white guy.

The other black guys, I found out, stayed in people's homes or boarding houses in a different part of town. Yeah, segregation was alive and very real. Blacks weren't welcome at the Haines City Hotel, but they never knew, I guess, that I was black. I stayed there through spring training.

I enjoyed a very successful Spring Training. I worked hard and I performed well, and I became somewhat of a hot commodity among the minor league managers. The Yankees used a system that spring that allowed the various minor league managers to choose the players for their teams. I believe this was the only time the Yankees ever did that. The manager of the Greensboro Yankees, Vern Rapp, a man who would one day manage in the Major Leagues for the St. Louis Cardinals, took a liking to my playing and he chose me. This was a B-level team, pretty high up the minor league ladder and a tough place for a player to begin his professional career. I would be up against a host of guys who had been playing for a few years. A bunch of future Major Leaguers were in that league including Rusty Staub, Rico Petrocelli, Tommie Agee, Cesar Tovar, Ed Brinkman, and Tony Perez. Tony Perez was a future Hall of Famer, but of course, he was just a kid at the time. Also in that league were a number of future teammates of mine. Ron Woods was there. As was Gene Michael and John Kennedy. Some of my teammates on that Greensboro team who made it to the Yankees were Curt Blefary, Frank Fernandez, and Mel Stottlemyre.

The bus ride from Florida's Spring Training to Greensboro, North Carolina took about eleven hours. This time, once we arrived, I also was a target of segregation. As we pulled up to the hotel, Vern Rapp said, "Hey Roy, you and Jim (a teammate from Puerto Rico) wait here on the bus." Eventually a taxi came and took us to where we would stay in the other part of town. The black players stayed in private homes away from the rest of the team. I stayed with a great person, Hezekiah Day. He would talk to me about the Negro Leagues. He'd even come to our games and give me advice on how to improve my game. It would be two to three years before I'd ever stay in the same hotel again with my teammates.

But there I was, a member of the Greensboro Yankees. I felt I was ready to compete, but I did not get off to a great start. Vern Rapp wanted me to change my swing and hit down on the ball. This wasn't my natural style, but he knew I was fast, and he was trying to make me into a ballplayer in the image of the great Maury Wills of the Dodgers. That may have been Wills' style, but it didn't work for me. Because of this, I struggled.

And Vern Rapp, I must say, was not the best manager for a first-year player, especially one far from home, just learning to be a pro, and facing a society the likes which he had never seen before. Rapp didn't take losing well. And we had a bad team. (The 1962 Greensboro Yankees played to a 65-75 record and finished the season 24 games behind the first place Durham Bills. Only two teams in the league finished with worse records.) The only time we'd win was when Mel Stottlemyre pitched. He was way ahead of everyone else down there.

After a loss, Rapp would be screaming in his office and throwing things. Then he'd come into the locker room and curse us all out and say we'd have to play better and all that. Most of us were terrified of him because he had such a bad temper. If this was how all of professional baseball was managed, I certainly didn't like it. I began to think about my future in the game. But I went out, played second base, tried to do my thing, tried to follow my manager's orders, and I struggled throughout.

In that league, I really got to see what talented ballplayers looked like and played like. Tommie Agee was an opposing player who scared me to death when he was on the bases. He'd have no problem taking you out at second base. When he was running, he was like a freight train or like thunder—the ground actually shook. I could feel him running. He was that strong. Agee had been a top football player. I was quick around the bag though, and he never got me.

After a few weeks (about 25 games), I was hitting only .204 and I was sent down to Ft. Lauderdale. This was D-Ball, so I was actually sent down two levels, but, in a way, it was like a promotion. The ballpark in Ft. Lauderdale was used by the New York Yankees as their Spring Training facility. We played in a new stadium that had a good infield so there were no bad hops there unlike the Greensboro field. The lighting was also great. We could see the ball much better at night. Small things like this often make a huge difference.

At this time, I was still a second baseman. The tough thing for a ball player is that once you get sent down (or up), you take another player's spot. In the minors, often times, once you take a guy's position, that spells the end of a guy's career and his dreams. For Ft. Lauderdale, I took the spot of a player named Dolph Camilli. (Camilli had batted .188 in 15 games.) His dad had been a power hitter in the National League with the Brooklyn Dodgers for years and was the National League Most Valuable Player in 1941. It's sad when you see a guy get released, especially when it is because of you.

My roommate in Ft. Lauderdale was Tony Anglada. I shared an apartment with him and his wife. Tony was a knuckleball pitcher from the Dominican Republic who didn't speak any English. He was 21 years old, but he seemed a lot older to the rest of us, and he taught me a lot about being a professional ballplayer.

Unlike the Greensboro squad, the 1962 Fort Lauderdale Yankees were a good team. We were fighting for a pennant. My own start there, though, didn't begin all that well. I was hitting about .230 or .240 and I started having doubts if I was good enough. In my mind, I had already failed at Greensboro, Level-B, and now I was struggling at Level-D. I wondered about what kind of job I'd have if I wasn't a ballplayer. In a way, in a big way, baseball was all I knew. In retrospect, I think every ballplayer goes through this—there is a period of time when things don't go right or well, and the competition just seems too good. We look at ourselves and we feel we just don't measure up.

The results weren't there at the start for me at Fort Lauderdale. Even when I'd do the right thing at bat, the balls, even when I hit them hard, just didn't fall. Everything I hit seemed to be caught. The players would kid me as the unluckiest guy around. I'd hit two or three line drives a game and none of them would go for hits. It went on like this for weeks. I laughed along with the guys, but inside it was eating me up.

But then, eventually, and finally, the hits started coming. My average got up to .250, then .260, and eventually all the way up to .280. Pretty soon I was leading the team in batting.

In one game, everything went right. I went five-for-five using five different bats. I would end up batting .286 that year. The only regular with a higher batting average at season's end was another future Yankee, Mike Hegan, who batted .306.

The 1962 Florida State League was a nice league of players. There were a lot of good players there that year: Bert Campaneris, Fergie Jenkins (a future Hall of Famer), Alex Johnson, Lee May, Jimmy Wynn, and Tommie Agee. Future Hall of Fame manager Tony LaRussa was a player in the league back then!

One of my best memories from that season was a game we played against Daytona Beach, a farm club for the Kansas City A's. Bert Campaneris was on that team. In a game against us, he played all nine positions in the field, something he would do again in the Major Leagues years later. The amazing thing, even more amazing than playing all nine positions, was that when he pitched, he pitched both left-handed and right-handed. Since I was a switch-hitter, I didn't know what he'd do when I batted. Would we both keep switching? Well, I got up left-handed and he stayed right-handed. I then hit a triple off him. Many years later we met at a dinner, and he said, "Roy, I should have thrown lefty to you."

That year we often traveled on a Checker Aerobus with various players taking turns driving. The team had about three of these. Because I was often the driver, they let me keep one to drive myself and Tony Anglada to the ballpark and around the city.

Some of these rides to the away games were five to six hours away. To entertain ourselves on the long rides, we'd do word games, tell jokes, or play "name that tune." The travel was at times tedious, but it served a valuable purpose in that we really got to know each other as teammates. The rides brought us closer together. We made the best of it and, as I look back, I realize that we had a lot of fun on those drives. We also learned a lot about each other. We had players on the team who came from New York City who told me about what life was like in the city and on the East Coast. This kind of information helped me a great deal when I finally made it to the big leagues.

Because of segregation, my non-white teammates and I couldn't stay with the team in the regular hotel and instead had to stay in the black section of town. The hotel where we stayed at home had a band, a loud band, that played every night. Our rooms were located just above where the band played. Needless to say, we didn't get much rest. So much of this life was new to all of us. We couldn't sleep, but we weren't sure how safe it was at night out on the streets. I, for one, never ventured out. After the games, I'd go right to my room.

Segregation also found its way to the ballpark. It was everywhere in the South back then. The stadium even had separate seating for the "colored fans." The black fans had to sit way down by the bullpen. I learned a lot about how different people view others.

That year we finished in first place with a 71-50 record. In spite of the challenges I faced professionally and societally, I learned a great deal. One of the most important lessons I learned was that I could play professional baseball and hold my own. The question I needed to answer was if I was good enough to get all the way to the big leagues.

***

In 1963, after a solid Spring Training. I returned to Level-B ball in Greensboro. That year, in Spring Training, there was no mistake about who I was. Along with Leroy Reams and the other black players, we stayed in the segregated part of town. There wasn't a nice hotel for us. Instead, we lived in a five-bedroom boarding house.

By now, I had grown more comfortable being away from home and found there was one benefit to living in the black section of the town—there was no curfew. There were no coaches who came to our section of the town to do bed checks or anything like that. We were on our own. During the season, we were focused on baseball and trying to get better so we could reach the big leagues. But I do recall in Spring Training, my teammates and I knowing we could do as we pleased, at least within reason. That often meant going to the local schools to watch basketball games or finding a court and playing ourselves into the night. We had some players who could really handle the ball and shoot well. I had a good shot but wasn't that great at dribbling and some of the other aspects of the game. Still, it was fun, and it brought us together.

I had a better time that year. I knew my way around the league a bit and had refined my game. I also brought a new level of confidence with me and felt that I was able to play at that level. Vern Rapp was no longer the manager, so I was able, without any push-back, to return to my natural swing. Frank Verdi was the manager of that team, and he was good to play for. He had a much more low-key approach. He wasn't as temperamental as Rapp had been. Verdi had been an infielder and he taught me a lot. I hit over .300 that year (.309) and I made the All-Star team.

My roommate that year was Jim Horsford. He was a black player from Puerto Rico. Horsford had been around a while. He had been playing minor league ball since 1957. He taught me a lot about the racism I was facing by sharing what he and so many others had to go through. It wasn't easy. Ever. Jim was a pitcher (and sometimes an outfielder). He also shared that he once beaned and killed a batter in a game. Because of that he had a lot to deal with. I was learning that there was a lot more to baseball than just the game. Jim never made it to the Major Leagues. He got close, making it to Triple-A. He eventually played in the Mexican League. Ballplayers are shuttled throughout a team's system. The Yankees had seven minor league teams in 1963 and six in 1964. I didn't see him again after that season.

We had a good team again. We won our division (going 85-59). Curt Blefary, who would win the Rookie of the Year with the Orioles in 1965, was a star on that team. He hit 25 homers and batted .290.

There were a bunch of great players in that league also. Joe Morgan, a future Hall of Famer, was there. Other future big leaguers who stand out were Lee May, Walt Williams, and Cleon Jones. Gene Michael and Lou Piniella were two long-time future teammates who I competed against. Luis Tiant, also just a kid, pitched in that league, but he was way ahead of us skill-wise. He should have been in the big leagues already.

By now, I was very comfortable as a professional baseball player, but that didn't mean that playing in the South at that time was pleasant. Oftentimes, mostly on the road, racist fans would yell at us on the field. I recall numerous times warming up in the on deck circle and hearing fans yelling "Hey LeRoy (not Roy, my name), if you get a hit, we're going to hang you after the game." It sure made me think. Another of the familiar racial epitaphs yelled at me when I was batting was the all-too-familiar refrain after my name was called by the public address announcer, "Now batting, Roy White." Certain fans would hear that and respond, "That ain't true."

Yes, racism was alive, and it is something I faced and had to live with on a daily basis. I was able to rise above it and perform. That doesn't mean it was easy. I found an inner strength and the taunts only made me stronger. I knew that the players who came before me, guys like Jackie Robinson and Larry Doby, and so many others, had it worse.

***

In 1964, I took another step closer to the big leagues as I reached Double-A with the Confederate Yankees who played in Columbus, Georgia. That team name today seems amazing. I can't imagine a team getting the name "Confederate Yankees" today. But, in 1964, I didn't think much of it. My job was to play ball.

Before that season started, I knew that I was a player the Yankees were watching. Before regular Spring Training opened, the Yankees had a special early camp in 1964. This was about a ten-day program designed for the top prospects to train with the big league Yankees. I was one of a handful of prospects, maybe fifteen in the whole system, to be invited to this early camp. Mel Stottlemyre and Mike Hegan, two future Major Leaguers, were also there with me.

I will never forget the first batting practice session that I watched. The early camp was, of course, at the Yankees' facility in Fort Lauderdale. At that park, there was a strong wind that blew from right field out to left. On windy days, it was all but impossible to hit the ball through that wind to get it out. The first batter to step into the batter's box and hit was Yogi Berra. He was the manager, but he still loved to hit. Each batter would lay down two bunts and then get eight swings. Yogi drove line drives all over the park. The next batter was Roger Maris. He actually hit one through that tough wind and over the right field wall. Mickey Mantle followed and then hit three balls out. I then watched Joe Pepitone stepping up. Joe hit five balls through that wind and over the wall. Five. These were bullets hit right through the wind. Pepitone had the quickest hands and swing I had ever seen. His batting stance, hitting in a sort-of crouch, reminded me of Stan Musial. The talent that I observed was eye-opening. These were big leaguers.

In that camp, the Yankees issued me uniform number 78. I wore it proudly even though such a high number signified that I was a long way from making the big squad.

Out on the field, Yankee greats Bobby Richardson and Jerry Coleman provided personal instruction to me about how to properly play second base. I saw how Richardson used one of those old flat, pancake-like gloves to transfer the ball quickly to his throwing hand to make a double play.

During that camp, we all stayed at the Yankee Clipper Hotel which was right on the beach. I'm not sure why the segregation rules didn't apply then. Maybe it was because we were big leaguers (or top prospects working to get there).

Double-A was a big step forward, but I felt I was ready. My manager that year was Rube Walker who had been a catcher for the Brooklyn Dodgers and would later be a Major League pitching coach for about twenty years. In fact, Rube was the pitching coach for the 1969 Miracle Mets. He was another great manager for me. I found that we, as players, thrived when the manager would support us and if we needed directives, he would criticize us gently. I knew that Rube was on my side. This helped more than one might imagine.

There were a lot of players more experienced than me in this league, some real talent. Frank Fernandez, a catcher with whom I'd play with the Yankees, was there. Mike Hegan, our first baseman, would also make it and have a fine career. These were two players I was climbing the minor league ladder with. At that time, I was still playing second base, my transition to the outfield was still in the future. Joe Faraci was my double play partner, our shortstop. We made a good combination.

Another infielder on the team was Ronnie Retton. He was a smaller guy, a Freddie Patek type player. He played hard. "Gutsy" would describe him. The 1964 season though was his last in pro ball. Years later, I met his daughter, the famous Olympic Gold Medal gymnast, Mary Lou Retton at a dinner. We were seated next to each other. She knew who I was and shared that I had played ball with her dad. It's amazing the small world connections I'd encounter over the course of my career. Years and years later, when I was a coach with the Yankees, a young shortstop named Bobby Meacham said, "You played ball for my dad." At first, I wondered what he was talking about, but then remembered Coach Meacham from when I was a kid playing junior high baseball.

I quickly acclimated to AA ball and was having a good season. I was hitting close to .300 and was on my way to the All-Star game in early July when everything suddenly changed. It happened on the ballfield. We were playing a game against the Macon Peaches, an affiliate of the Cincinnati Reds. It was a Sunday afternoon. I hit a slow chopper to third and hustled down the line to beat it out. The third baseman, I believe it was Len Boehmer, did not make an accurate throw and the ball came inside the first base line at the exact moment as I was running hard to the bag. The first baseman, Lee May, was also arriving at that exact moment. Lee May was a big strong man who would go on to have a long and successful career with the Cincinnati Reds and the Baltimore Orioles. His elbow hit me square on the left side of my face. I went down immediately, knocked out, unconscious.

The next thing I knew I was on the ground being put on a stretcher and brought to the clubhouse. The doctor looked at me and said it was just a bad bruise, that I'd have a black eye, but I'd be okay. Subsequent happenings proved that that doctor was very wrong.

After the game, back at my apartment, the pain was bad. Excruciating. My face was throbbing. I had to take seven or eight Tylenol just to get to sleep. The next morning, I woke up with my face really swollen. I looked like Frankenstein. We had a road trip to Knoxville starting at about 8:00 a.m. I told Rube Walker, "I think it's more than just a black eye." He said that he'd get me checked out at the hospital when we reached Knoxville. That 10-hour bus ride was interminable. I felt every bump in my face. It was excruciating. And worse.

Once at Knoxville, I first tried to suit up for the game, but I knew I couldn't play. I couldn't run. Everything hurt too much. I was soon at the hospital getting an X-Ray. The doctor who checked me out stated that that the rim of my eye socket in my left eye had a fracture and that I needed an operation. He noted that I could get double vision if it wasn't repaired. Double vision would, of course, have spelled the end of my baseball career. The doctor stated that he could do the surgery, a painful procedure that would have had him drill a hole just above my gum line to drain my sinus of blood and then stuff it with cotton, the next day.

I went back to the team and told Rube Walker what the doctor suggested. Rube told me that he'd call the Yankees to see what they wanted me to do. Since I was able to fly, they had me come to New York City to be evaluated at Lenox Hill Hospital. Fortunately I was a legitimate prospect and doing well because the Yankees were making sure that I was going to get the very best care.

This was my first ever trip to New York. I reported to Yankee Stadium and went into the clubhouse. I remember Tommy Tresh coming over to welcome me. Then the other guys too. I looked pretty bad with a swollen and bruised face. They all asked what had happened. I stayed for the game, one in which the Yankees won in the late innings against the Baltimore Orioles who were in first place. Tom Tresh hit an RBI single off Stu Miller to score Mickey Mantle in the bottom of the eighth inning to give the Yankees the lead.

Later, at Lenox Hill Hospital, they determined that I did not need an operation. I was admitted and they fixed the swelling and the drainage issue without surgery. Three days later I was out of the hospital and back on my way to the minor leagues. But, for that year, at least, I wasn't the same player.

A big part of the problem was that it was a few weeks before I could even eat solid food. This impacted my energy and fitness. I was somewhat miserable. As a result, I struggled at the plate and my batting average dropped. What had been such a promising season ended disappointingly. My final batting average that season was only .253.

At one point that year, a promotion to Triple-A seemed a very real possibility, but following the injury, because of my slump, I never got that promotion.

***

In 1965, I returned to Columbus for what would be my last full minor league season. This time everything worked out great. There is a lesson here in believing in oneself and the value of perseverance. I knew I was a better player than the one that slumped to a finish in 1964. I worked hard and was determined to be better the next year. Plus, I was healthy. In baseball, the law of averages also seems to play a role. In my first minor league season, everything I hit seemed to get caught. In 1965, everything I hit seemed to fall in. I was hitting everything they threw up there. I stayed consistent throughout the whole year.

I remember a series we played in Chattanooga that year against the Lookouts. In that series, I must have had 12 hits in 18 at bats including two or three home runs. They just couldn't get me out. Not long after that, we were back in Columbus playing a home series again against the Lookouts. I continued my hot hitting. This prompted their manager, the former Phillies catcher Andy Seminick, to yell out to his pitcher as I came up to bat, "Tell him what's coming. It can't be any worse." The pitcher said "Fastball." I didn't know what to expect and he threw a fastball right by me. It seemed he was telling the truth so when he next yelled "Curveball," I was ready. I hit that one off the right centerfield wall for a triple. After that they went back to not telling me what pitches were coming.

We had a great team that year. A host of future Yankees played on the 1965 Confederate Yankees. Frank Fernandez was there, as was Mike Hegan. But we also had Steve Whitaker, Mike Ferraro, and a few others. Our pitching staff had two solid starters who each had Major league success, Fritz Peterson and Stan Bahnsen. Peterson would win 20 games in 1970 and was an All-Star. Bahnsen would be the 1968 American League Rookie of the Year.

We had a great manager that year, Loren Babe. Hall of Fame manager Tony LaRussa would later give Loren Babe credit for teaching him how to manage. He was a manager who simply understood the game and the players. Like the good managers I'd encounter before and after, we knew he cared about us. He believed in us, and we worked hard to reward his confidence with our best play. Loren Babe would later coach at the big league level with the Yankees and the White Sox.

In my minor league days, there was a roving hitting coach for the Yankees named Wally Moses. He helped my career significantly. Because I was often hitting well, he didn't work with me often. He was always with the other guys, the players who might have been struggling. Then, one day, he came up to me and said, "Roy, just because I haven't talked to you, that doesn't mean I haven't been watching you. The main thing is you have one problem—sometimes you wait too long and then try to be quick all at once. This brings you out of your crouch too fast and you don't get a quality swing." He advised me to, "get started early." In other words, to be better prepared to hit before the ball was out of the pitcher's hand. This was great advice that I used my entire career. It's also advice that I shared with others when I was a coach myself. It helped numerous players including a bunch of stars—guys like Don Mattingly and even Derek Jeter. The way I helped Jeter was indirect and it's a story I'll get to later.

That year, our team finished in a tie for first place with the Asheville Tourists. It was a strong league with dozens of future Major Leaguers playing against us on a daily basis. Pat Dobson, John Hiller, and Mike Marshall, all who had a good deal of big league success all pitched against us.

That year I hit .300 along with 19 homers. I also scored 103 runs—all while batting lead-off. I was named the Most Valuable Player of the Southern League. It was a great season all around.

After the 1965 minor league season ended, Loren Babe called me to his office and said, "Forget your ticket home to Los Angeles. You got a call to play for the Yankees."

My Major League career was about to begin!

Playing with Roy White
in the Minor Leagues
By Ian Dixon

Ian Dixon, a third baseman initially, and later a pitcher, was a minor leaguer in the New York Yankees system from 1961 through 1964. In 1962, he played in Greensboro and Ft. Lauderdale with Roy White. They also played together in 1963 at Greensboro.

***

I FIRST MET ROY in 1962 during Spring Training. Roy came in as a rookie. I am about a year older and had played a bit the previous summer with St. Petersburg. I had lived the professional baseball player's life for about a month and a half. In our world at that time, and with our experiences, that made me the older veteran.

People might think of Spring Training as a relaxing experience for the players, that we do some light stretches in the Florida sun and then do some calisthenics and play some ball. It is not like that at all, or wasn't for us. Spring Training was a long and arduous process. As an infielder, we were out on the field, in the hot Florida sun, from 9:30 in the morning, often until 4:00 in the late afternoon.

Roy and I met at one of the lunch breaks as we ate sandwiches and drank juice. It was easy to talk and be with Roy. He was very down to earth. We started chatting and found that we both liked to play basketball and had a few other things in common.

You also get to know a player when you play with him on

the field, for hours and hours. We practiced double plays time and again, for weeks. It was my job, as the third baseman, to grab the ball and get it to Roy at second base quickly so he could catch it and throw the ball before being killed by the base runner. What I liked about Roy was that he was always there. I knew exactly where to throw the ball, even if I didn't see him yet, I knew he'd be there. He was that quick. I'd throw the ball to a location, and he'd appear to catch it and turn the double play. Some things just click, and this did. We felt each other's baseball rhythm. In a way, it was like being in a band. We just knew what the other guy was going to do. And we got along great.

At the end of that first Spring Training, they posted our assignments in a gymnasium inside the complex. I saw that we were both going to Greensboro, which was a big jump for me and a huge jump for Roy as he was a mere rookie. Eventually, not very long in fact, we both got sent down a step to Ft. Lauderdale which was, in some ways, a promotion because that ballpark was so nice.

The Ft. Lauderdale park was where the Major League Yankees trained. The lighting was great. The infield was smooth like a billiard table. It was a beautiful park. The Yankees also loaded that team with great talent since this was their first year having a minor league team there. The community loved us. It was great. In the end, we beat future Hall of Famer Fergie Jenkins to win the championship.

Roy White was a great player on that team. He was a switch hitter, of course. He was a contact hitter with a short swing. He also had more power than he realized. Because of the short swing, he didn't strike out much. He was speedy, he made contact, and it was clear that he could really play. Unfortunately, he got off to a slow start down there—everything he hit turned into an out. The soft hits were outs, and even the balls he hit on the nose were turned into outs. The guys gave him a hard time in the dugout. They wouldn't touch him or his bat hoping to make sure that his slump and bad luck didn't rub off on them. Eventually he started hitting and he didn't stop from that point on. He hit well over .300 from mid-June to the end of the season. What impressed me about Roy, something that's always been true of him, was his character. He stayed positive. He never lost confidence.

Roy also had to battle something I didn't. As a white guy from Canada, I did not experience the racism of the South in the early 1960s. Roy never lived any of that in Compton—the segregated seating at the ballparks, the separate water fountains, and more. It was a different world. It wasn't easy to see this, and to live it, but I never heard Roy complain.

I always felt that a good person was a good person. A person's color didn't matter to me, and it still doesn't matter. If you're a good guy, you're a good guy. And Roy White became my lifelong friend because he is a good guy.

After that first year, we were sure we'd be promoted again, and, after Spring Training in 1963, we were. Roy and I found ourselves in that same gym, looking at the rosters and seeing that we'd both be going to Greensboro. I asked Roy how he was getting there. He figured he'd have to take the team bus. That year I had my car, purchased from my bonus money. I had driven it, a beautiful red Chevy Impala with a white top, whitewall tires, and a white stripe down the side, all the way to Florida from my home on the west coast of Canada. That car was a beauty, and it turned heads. I said to Roy, "You come with me. We will drive up to Greensboro together."

Now, this wasn't as easy as it sounds. This was 1963 and we'd be driving, a white guy and a black guy, in an eye-catching car through the racial hotbed that was the South. I wanted to do this, but it was something we had to discuss together. Mixed races just didn't drive together in those days. But we had a plan. I figured if we stayed on the freeways, we'd be away from some of the more radical areas. I also said that we'd only stop at places right off the highways and that I would be the guy to go into the restaurants to get any food. Roy would hang back in the car. I told him, if you think any trouble is coming, I have a blanket in the back, and to climb under it to get out of sight. That never had to happen. That ride we took has been written about often. It was a memorable experience. It brought us even closer together and formed much of the cement of our 60-year friendship.

I left the game to go to university after the 1964 season, but Roy, of course, kept playing. We were able to keep in touch. When Roy went to Spokane, he called me, and we got together.

In 1969, when the Yankees would play in Seattle against the Pilots, I'd go down and see him and Mel Stottlemyre, who had once been my roommate. I remember calling to Roy once from the stands and hearing him say, "Ian Dixon, I'd know that voice anywhere." By 1969, of course, Roy was a star. He was never too big for his friends, or really anyone though. A great word to describe Roy White is gentlemanly.

After playing for the Yankees, Roy went to play in Japan. We'd see each other from time to time. Roy shared his love of Japanese art with me. He brought me a beautiful piece that still hangs in my home.

When Roy coached in the Oakland A's system, his team was in Vancouver. I had an apartment over my garage that I offered for Roy to live in. That summer, we became closer, as a real family as our wives also became close friends. We spent a lot of time together. If the games ended early enough, Roy would come home with a bottle of wine and hold it up outside the window. I'd let him in, and we'd listen to great music and just have a great time.

I was able to come to New York in 2011. Roy took me all over. At Yankee Stadium, he is royalty. This is deservedly so. Roy White is a man of dignity and class. He is sensitive and understanding of others. New York is a tough town. Not many guys can survive there, but the fans loved him—still do. He played every day, he played hurt, and he did all the things needed to do to win. He could hit, walk, steal a base, take the extra base, make great catches.

Roy was also loved in Japan. They still remember him as the most respected North American ballplayer to ever play in Japan.

There are few people in this world as dignified as Roy White. It's especially difficult to find people like Roy in professional sports. There is no one better than Roy White, a quiet gentleman.

I am very fortunate to call him my friend.

Chapter 3
...To The Bronx
My First Big League Experience
1965

AND THERE I WAS, for the second time in my life, walking into the Yankees' clubhouse. Only this time I wasn't just an injured minor leaguer visiting the big squad. I was now a legitimate member of the team. I was a New York Yankee. I remember seeing my locker and my uniform hanging there. It was a special moment. This was the same locker room where Babe Ruth, Lou Gehrig, and Joe DiMaggio had changed. My clothes were in the same lockers that they, and countless other stars, had used.

Pete Sheehy was the man who ran the clubhouse in the original Yankee Stadium. He had been there since the days of Babe Ruth and was a legend himself. It was Sheehy's job to issue the players their uniform numbers. I was issued number 48. I wore that number for the first few years of my career. I also wore number 21 briefly. Today people know me for the number 6 that I wore throughout most of my career, but I didn't get that uniform number until 1969.

As I entered the clubhouse, congratulations from the other players came. "Good to see you," "Welcome," and such. It was great. I remember the younger guys, especially, welcoming me to the team. This included Tom Tresh, Phil Linz, and Jim Bouton. The great Elston Howard, the first African American to play for the Yankees, just two years removed from his MVP season also welcomed me.

The date was September 7, 1965. The Yankees were in

sixth place (in the ten team American League) with a record of 68-73 and they were playing out the string for the first time in decades. The Yankees had reached the World Series (there were no playoffs back then) in fourteen of the previous sixteen seasons. The only years since 1949 when the Yankees were not in the World Series were 1954 and 1959. And now, 1965. I don't think anyone remembered a season when the Yankees had previously finished under .500. (This would be the first time since 1925, the year of Babe Ruth's famous bellyache, that the Yankees would finish a season with more losses than wins.)

Johnny Keane was the Yankees manager. He had managed against the Yankees in the previous year's World Series and had led the St. Louis Cardinals to the World Championship. Now he was the manager of the Yankees and things were not going so well.

I remember that the Yankees were playing the Baltimore Orioles that day. The Orioles were in the pennant race, so these were serious games. It was a Tuesday doubleheader. The first game had been rescheduled to that day due to a rainout a few weeks prior.

In addition to sitting in the clubhouse and on the bench with some of the greatest Yankees of all time, Mickey Mantle, Roger Maris, Elston Howard, and others, I remember looking across the field at the great players on the Orioles: Brooks Robinson, Luis Aparicio, Boog Powell and thinking, "I had the baseball cards of some of these guys, and now I am here!" My former minor league teammate Curt Blefary was also on that Orioles squad. He was on his way to winning the Rookie of the Year Award that year. That was a solid Orioles team that would finish in third place in 1965, but they were about to arrive. The next year, 1966, they would win the World Series.

Al Downing, a young left-hander, was pitching for us in the first game of the doubleheader against Dave McNally of the Orioles. I was enjoying just taking it all in when, in the bottom of the seventh inning, Johnny Keane yelled down, "Roy, grab a bat. You're hitting for Downing."

I never thought I'd actually get into the game!

As I was getting ready, Elston Howard came over to me and started giving me a scouting report of what to expect from Dave McNally. Then, not before very long, I heard Bob Sheppard's voice on the Yankee Stadium PA system, *"Now batting for the Yankees... number 48... Roy White...number 48."*

I was terrified. 30,000 fans were in attendance. I had never before played for more than a few thousand. McNally was a left-handed pitcher, so I got up batting right-handed. There were two outs and we were losing to the Orioles 4-0.

I went to the plate and used what I called my Dick Allen stance. I used to copy the batting stances of successful big leaguers. Dick Allen was a star. McNally pitched me just as Elston Howard had predicted—the first two pitches were fastballs that tailed away. The first one I fouled back. The second one I took for a strike. Now, according to Howard's quick scouting report, I knew I should expect a curve ball down and in, but McNally threw me another fastball. It was almost past me, I didn't want to go down looking, so I swung, it was almost a reflex action, and hit a line drive right through the middle for a base hit. In my first Major League at bat, I singled. I still have that baseball.

Bobby Richardson then singled me to third and I scored on a base hit by Tom Tresh. We ended up losing that game 4-2. Don Larsen, a decade removed from his World Series perfect game, and now in his last full Major League season, pitched in relief for the Orioles that game.

In the second game of the doubleheader, Johnny Keane put me in as the starting second baseman. Not only that, I was to be the Yankees' leadoff hitter. In that game we were facing Wally Bunker who had been the Rookie of the Year the season before.

I had two hits against Bunker, a ground-rule double, and a single. After the single, I scored on a ground out again by Tom Tresh. I remember Mickey Mantle saying to me, "There's nothing to this game, is there?"

***

I appeared in 14 games that first season. I had 14 hits

in 42 at bats for a .333 batting average. I scored seven runs, walked four times, and stole two bases. These are the attributes I would be known for throughout my career. I was a player who hit well, got on base a lot (I took my fair share of walks), could steal bases, and I also scored a lot of runs.

I also became known as a pretty good outfielder who had a weak arm. It's time I explained all of that since those changes also happened that season.

As a kid playing American Legion ball and through the minor leagues, I was always an infielder. I played a little shortstop, but I mostly played second base. Just a few days into my big league career, at White Sox Park in Chicago, Johnny Keane told me to take some flies in the outfield during batting practice.

The next thing I knew, I was put into the lineup as the starting right fielder. Bobby Murcer was also a rookie that year, and he was penciled in as the shortstop. Since the White Sox were in the pennant race, Johnny Keane didn't want to put two novice infielders in the lineup in the same game. He didn't want to make it look like the Yankees weren't trying. As a result, I went to the outfield.

I was terrified out there. I had never played outfield as a professional and I hadn't played right field since the earliest days of my Little League experience. That was, of course, the spot where they put the worst player. I knew that wasn't the case in the big leagues—every position mattered. Inning after inning, though, no balls were hit my way. In the bottom of the fifth inning, Tommy John, the White Sox pitcher, flew out to me in right field. In the next inning, Don Buford, a speedy outfielder, lined a base hit to right field. I raced over to the gap to field the ball and tried to hump up to make a strong throw to second base to keep Buford to a single. It was a good throw. Buford remained at first, but I felt a twinge in my right shoulder. My arm, amazingly, would never be the same.

Back then players, especially rookies, didn't complain of soreness or pulled muscles. Actions like that were seen as signs of weakness. The clubhouse medicine of the time included a rub down or just shrugging it off. That's what we did back then. It was expected that players play through pain and even some injuries. Today they would have probably diagnosed me with some sort of tendonitis or a torn muscle and been able to fix it, but back then, we just played through the discomfort or pain. Previously I had had a pretty strong arm, but it would never be the same again.

We also had one of the greatest role models of all time in regard to playing through pain right in our locker room—Mickey Mantle. By the time I reached the Yankees, Mickey Mantle was a fading star, but he was still a baseball legend. Mantle was just 33 years old in 1965, but he wasn't the player he had been. That year he failed to hit .300 (he hit .255) or hit 30 home runs (he hit just 19). We were also out of the pennant race, but still, no one played harder than the Mick. He ran everything out. He gave every game everything he had.

I remember a doubleheader that we played late in the 1968 season. We were in Washington playing the Senators. I watched in the clubhouse before the games as Mickey Mantle was being taped up. It seemed every single muscle in his body was hurt. Yet there he was, getting wrapped so that he could play ball. I'm not sure if he knew it at the time, but this would be Mantle's last Major League season. The Yankees were again out of the race, and Mickey, of course, had nothing left to prove. Yet, there he was, in great pain, doing everything he could to be able to play. I also remember it being very warm that day.

On that day, with only a few weeks left in his career, Mickey Mantle played both ends of the doubleheader. He played the entirety of both games. We won both games. Mantle hit a two-run double in the first game to propel us to the victory.

After watching Mickey Mantle's example of strength and courage, I knew that a standard had been set. How could I ever not play hard? This was how champions played. I resolved to always be that type of player.

Chapter 4
My Early Years in the Big Leagues
1966-1967

AFTER FINDING SUCCESS AS a Major League Baseball player in 1965, I was especially looking forward to the 1966 season. I had reached the big leagues after playing most of the 1965 season at Double-A. I felt that the 1966 season was going to be my chance to earn a spot in Spring Training to stay with the big team all season long. I felt that my time as a Major League ballplayer had arrived.

That Spring Training, I was getting to play a lot. It seemed that the Yankees had confidence in me and wanted to see what they had in me—what type of ballplayer I was. Throughout the exhibition season, I was playing some second base, but I was also playing some outfield. Remarkably, I was even playing a bit of center field. This was a big deal. That spring, Mickey Mantle was being converted to a first baseman. The Yankees, for the first time in a very long time, needed a centerfielder. I was among the candidates being considered for that role.

Looking back, I was very fortunate to get that chance. Way back, in 1936, the great Joe DiMaggio took over the position, and except for the years during World War II, he held that spot until he retired after the 1951 season. The next year, Mickey Mantle took over in center. Even though he was getting older and slower, and even though he played mostly in left field in 1965, the feeling was that centerfield was still Mickey Mantle's. A new era was dawning, and at times I was the man playing in the large shadows of DiMaggio and Mantle.

It was a thrill to report to Spring Training as a Yankee. My wife Linda came with me. Of course, we still couldn't get an apartment with the other players and had to stay in the black section of town. We stayed in a small house that we shared with Ellie Rodriguez, an up-and-coming catcher who would play briefly for the Yankees and would play for numerous teams over his nine-year career. Ellie's wife was pregnant and didn't feel well so we never had much of a chance, other than in the car rides to the ballpark, to get close.

I played hard, worked hard, and performed well that spring. At the end of Spring Training, I was honored with the James P. Dawson Award as the best rookie in camp. But many players who are regarded as the best rookies in camp are still not ready for the Major Leagues. Many are sent to Double-A or Triple-A for more experience. That wasn't the case with me though. I soon found out that I made the cut and would be heading north with the big club.

This was an exciting time. I felt good about my abilities, and I was performing well against the best competition. Some sports writers even said that I might be a strong candidate for the American League Rookie of the Year Award. Things were looking that great!

I appeared in the game on Opening Day coming up in a big spot as a pinch hitter in the bottom of the ninth inning, at Yankee Stadium, with our team down just 2-1. There were two outs, but we had runners on first and third. Clete Boyer was the runner at third, Joe Pepitone was on at first base. In that spot, Johnny Keane, our manager, sent me up to pinch hit for our shortstop Ruben Amaro.

I have always prided myself on my ability to drive in runs in big spots and to come through when needed. The previous year, in 1965, I came up three times as a pinch hitter, succeeding each time with two hits and a walk in those three plate appearances. I was expecting more of the same. I always had the ability to focus on the task at hand, especially in big spots. Unfortunately, on this occasion I was bested. Mickey Lolich, the terrific pitcher for the Tigers, got me to pop out to end the game.

But after that, I found myself on a roll. In our second game, I was the starting centerfielder. Mickey had started in center on Opening Day, but I was there for Game Two, batting second in the lineup.

We were facing another great pitcher, Denny McLain, but things just started rolling for me. I doubled in my first at bat and walked in three other plate appearances.

In the next game, I was called upon to pinch hit, and this time I delivered a single.

For the fourth game of the season, I was back in centerfield. I went 1-for-3. It was clear that I had my timing down early and was getting hits every time we played. I was soon playing regularly, often in centerfield. Johnny Keane saw me as a player in the mold of Curt Flood, the excellent outfielder on the St. Louis Cardinals. And I did not disappoint.

It was in our seventh game, a contest in which I went 3-for-4, that I hit my first big league home run. It came off Sam McDowell of the Cleveland Indians. I hit that shot batting right-handed putting the ball into the left field seats.

I homered again a few days later against Boston. And then I homered again a few days after that against Kansas City. By mid-May, my batting average was around .300 and I was hitting for power and driving in runs. Everything I hit, I was hitting hard. As I made my trek through the minor leagues, I always assumed that I had the talent and abilities to make it to the Major Leagues and perform well, but there's a big difference in believing that a person can do something and actually doing it. It was a great feeling to know that I was doing exactly what I believed I could.

I was hitting for more power, but I wasn't too surprised by this. In the off season, a few guys and I, the Compton ball players who were now professionals, worked out with weights at Compton Junior College. They had a nice gym there that we were able to use. We weren't lifting heavy stuff, but instead were doing exercises designed to build strength in our forearms, wrists, and hands. The days of baseball players bulking up and becoming muscle bound were decades in the future. Instead, we worked on muscle tone and flexibility. Instead of having bulging biceps we wanted strong quick hands and wrists. And all that work was paying off. I was among the

Yankees' team leaders in home runs and runs batted in.

And that was the start of my downfall...

I started thinking that I might hit 25-30 homers. I started to believe that I was a home run hitter. These were delusions of grandeur. I wasn't a home run hitter, but as I tried to become one, I went away from my natural swing. I should have known better because when I went away from my natural swing in the minor leagues, it didn't work. And it was destined not to work again. I was subconsciously trying to pull every pitch. As a result, I started popping up rather than driving the ball. My early success was working against me. In a way, I probably thought the Major Leagues were easier than they really were. The pitchers learned how to pitch me, and I was doing myself no favors by trying to hit every pitch over the wall.

By June, I was in a tailspin. My batting average just kept falling and falling. Back then, teams did not have hitting coaches. By and large, we, as professionals, were expected to figure it out. My teammates were always supportive saying things like, "The hits will come" and "hang in there." Hitting a baseball isn't easy, some say it's the most difficult thing in sports. All it takes is a slight change in one's hands or swing or step... or anything, to throw off an entire swing.

I remember my final games as a regular that season. The end started to come during a doubleheader at Yankee Stadium on June 21, I played both ends of that twin bill. We were playing the Orioles, a great team that would go on to win the World Series that year. In the first game, we were down 7-5 in the bottom of the 9th. I had already homered in the game, a good shot off Wally Bunker. Now I was up again with the game on the line. There were two outs. Tom Tresh was at second base, Bobby Richardson was on first. I hit a drive to deep right field off Stu Miller. I knew it had enough to go. The Orioles' right fielder was future Hall of Famer Frank Robinson. He went way back for the ball, but I was still sure it was gone. I even saw an umpire signal that it was a homer, but as I rounded second base, it seems that Robinson caught the ball as he fell into the stands. Our manager, Ralph Houk came out to argue, to no avail. Instead of a big day with two hits, both home runs, including the game winner, I was 1-for-5 in a game we lost. Worse yet, in the field, I made two errors. Both of those errors came in the second inning, and both on bad throws I made trying to gun out a runner trying to score. The Orioles scored five runs in that inning to take the lead that we never recaptured. I was booed as I ran off the field. I almost made up for those errors with the game winning home run, one that I hoped would jump start my season. But it wasn't a homer, and my season wasn't jump started.

In the second game of the doubleheader, I went 0-for-3. I batted eighth in the lineup that game, just in front of the pitcher. (These were the days before the designated hitter.) Earlier in the year, when I was hitting well, I was the number two hitter in the batting order batting right in front of Roger Maris or Mickey Mantle.

I just couldn't get it going. We still had two more games against the Orioles. I started those games and got just one hit in those two games to drop my batting average further. And it continued to get worse. After a road trip to Boston and Washington, D.C., a trip where I had just three hits in total, my batting average for the season sat at a miserable .221. Those were my last games as a starter that year.

I stayed on the big club, the Yankees didn't give up on me totally, but my playing time was more sporadic. It became a long season. It is very difficult to break out of a slump and to correct bad habits when one isn't playing regularly. That home run I hit on June 21 against the Orioles was the last one I hit all season. Where I once thought I might hit a ton of homers, my season ended with just the seven that I had hit early on. I ended up batting only .225 for the season, with those seven home runs and just 20 runs batted in.

There was no Rookie of the Year Award for me based on that showing. Tommy Agee, who I had played against in the minor leagues, and was such a force when I saw him running on the base paths, won the award while playing for the White Sox. Agee would soon become a New York Met and would be part of their famous championship team in 1969.

The Yankees as a team also did poorly. The 1966 Yankees

finished in last place in the American League—finishing in 10th place in a ten-team league. For the Yankees, this wasn't just bad, it was historically bad. The Yankees hadn't finished in last place since the days long before Mickey Mantle and Joe DiMaggio and even the days before Lou Gehrig and Babe Ruth. Until 1966, the Yankees hadn't finished in last place since 1912, back before they were ever even called the Yankees. Back in 1912, the franchise was called the Highlanders. That 1966 season was only the third time in the franchise's entire history that a Yankees (or Highlanders) team finished in last place. 1908 was the only other time that happened. I was part of a historical Yankees team, except that we were historically bad rather than historically great.

When I signed with the Yankees after high school, they were the team that always won. Year after year, the Yankees were in the World Series. Now, here I was, a member of the New York Yankees, just finishing my first season, and we weren't just not championship quality, we were the worst team in the entire league.

During the 1966 season, our manager Johnny Keane was fired. Ralph Houk, who had managed the Yankees from 1961 to 1963 and was currently the General Manager, returned to the dugout as the "new" manager. Johnny Keane had been a fine manager, but I felt that Ralph Houk was a great choice. The players loved Houk. He was a tough, smart, and very fair manager. In the years to come, I'd love playing for him.

That season was a lesson learned for me. I learned that I was not going to be a home run hitter. To remind myself of that fact, I began the practice of choking up on the bat. My main focus for the following seasons would be to not think about home runs, but to keep my swing short and compact and to use the whole field. To remind myself to not swing for the fences each time up, I would choke up about one inch to start each at bat. With two strikes on me, I'd choke-up even further, up to two or even three inches. This was a practice I followed for the rest of my career.

The 1966 season was a lost one for me, but the year 1966 itself did bring some happiness. After the season, I married my wife Linda to whom I have now been married for well over fifty years.

Linda and I had met the off-season before courtesy of my childhood friend Dave Kelly. Well, we met, at least indirectly, from Dave who had invested in a duplex in Inglewood. I'd often accompany him when he made visits there to do repairs or check on the building. One day we were talking to a guy downstairs who was impressed that he knew a couple of minor league ballplayers. He mentioned that he had a good-looking sister, who arrived at just about that time. That sister was Linda. She became my wife.

I was happily married, but I was also a baseball player, and because I did not have a good year and sat on the bench for most of the second half of the year, I needed to get some playing time. Sometimes there is no off-season. I headed off to Puerto Rico to play winter ball. This was high-level baseball. Most of the Latin stars of the time played in that league including future Hall of Famers Orlando Cepeda and Tony Perez. In addition, many other up-and-coming ballplayers including the likes of Steve Carlton, another future Hall of Famer, who would be my teammate, were also in the league that year. I was pleased that I would be playing against great competition. I needed to improve my skills and the only way to do that was to compete against the best players. I had suffered through a bad season. I was determined to get better and to be a quality big league ballplayer.

The Puerto Rican Winter League was comprised of six teams around the island. My team played out of Ponce. I once again found myself at second base. Horace Clarke, who played second base for the Yankees, was our shortstop. Our manager was Luis Arroyo who had been the Yankees ace relief pitcher on their famous 1961 World Championship squad.

This was a great experience for me. I played well, regaining some of the confidence I had lost during the long 1966 season. It was while I was down there that the Yankees made a shocking trade sending our star third baseman Clete Boyer to the Atlanta Braves. The Yankees sent word that I should start taking grounders at third base in pregame workouts. It looked to me that my position might be changing yet again when the 1967 season would roll around.

In Spring Training, I found that the Yankees had high hopes for me at third base. I started playing games there. The Yankees moved me around a lot that spring. I did well enough, even though I never felt great at third base. That position certainly wasn't in my comfort zone. Each position on a baseball field takes a certain skill set. A second baseman cannot just become a third baseman. At third, the ball comes off the bat much faster. That position is called the "hot corner" for a reason. A third baseman needs tremendous reflexes, like my future teammate Graig Nettles possessed. The angles and the paths that batted balls take also vary from position to position. I handled myself well enough, but I did not enjoy the Yankees' Spring Training experiment of having me play this new position.

I felt I did well enough in Spring Training to make the Major League club again, but on the final day, just as we were breaking camp, Pete Sheehy came over to me and said, "Ralph wants to see you." It is never a good sign when a player is called into the manager's office.

During the spring, the Yankees lost their shortstop, Ruben Amaro to injury. Once I was in Ralph Houk's office, he told me that since the Yankees needed a shortstop, they had to make a trade—and that I was the player being traded away in a unique arrangement with the Los Angeles Dodgers. Ralph then said, "The good news is we still own you, we have your rights, but you're going to play on loan for the Dodgers' farm team." I was part of the deal that the Yankees used to acquire John Kennedy to play shortstop for them. I guess the Dodgers thought that even though I was on loan, that I'd eventually stick with their club.

Instead of heading north with the Yankees to New York, I had to report to Vero Beach, Florida to the Dodgers' camp. I also had to call my wife Linda who was expecting me to arrive in Washington D.C. with the Yankees. Imagine making that call, "I'm not a Major Leaguer with the Yankees, I am a minor leaguer again now with the Dodgers." In many ways, I was completely deflated. The Dodgers were, of course, a great franchise. The Dodgers had won the 1963 World Series (over the Yankees) and the 1965 World Series as well. In 1966, they again were in the World Series, but they lost to the Orioles. As a franchise in that part of the 1960s, the Dodgers were having a whole lot more success than the Yankees. Still, it wasn't a good feeling to be traded or loaned away. It was a big step backwards in my career.

I reported to Vero Beach and was quickly assigned to the Dodgers' Triple-A minor league team, the Spokane Indians. Not long before, I was heading off to play in the nation's capital, but now I was on my way to the other Washington, the one on the west coast. Roy Hartsfield, the manager, welcomed me and gave me the next surprise. I was informed that I wasn't going to play second base because they already had a player named Nate Oliver there. Oliver had been up and down with the Dodgers for years. He'd eventually also play for the San Francisco Giants and the Chicago Cubs and one game for the Yankees in 1969. Hartsfield then said, "We need you at third."

I finished Spring Training with the Spokane team playing third base. We then flew on the Dodger team plane, first to Los Angeles, and then to Spokane. In Los Angeles, my wife Linda joined us, and she was able to spend the season with me. There were a lot of good players on that team. Twenty-two players from that Spokane team eventually made the big leagues. In addition to Nate Oliver, we had Tommy Hutton, Tommy Dean, Cleo James, and many others.

I wasn't thrilled to be back in the minor leagues. Spokane was a long way from New York, and it was even a long way from Los Angeles. The good news was that I tore the league up. Choking up on my bat, I hit .343. I also hit six home runs, although I wasn't swinging for them. I became comfortable at third base, partially because we had Tommy Hutton at first base, who caught everything I threw. I can't stress that enough. Hutton was remarkable. It's a long throw from third and often at a difficult angle, but no matter where I threw the ball or how I got it over to first, Hutton caught it. He saved me a lot of errors and made me look better than I was.

I made the All-Star team. We were in first place. Things were going well. I'm sure the Dodgers were very happy they had me. I believe they saw me as a player like the great Maury Wills. I could run, steal bases, and hit well. In some ways, I was the prototypical Dodgers-type player at the time. I'm certain they saw me as a future member of the team, but I wondered if there was a future in Los Angeles for me at third base. The Dodgers' big league third baseman in 1967 was Jim Lefebvre, one of the guys I played against in high school ball. I was certain that he would be playing third for the Dodgers for quite a long time.

Up to that point in my career, all of my minor league experiences had been in the south. Spokane was a completely different experience for me. There was no segregation. I didn't encounter racial taunts from the fans. Linda and I did have one experience there that we had never encountered before, growing up in Los Angeles and playing ball in the south, and in the north only in the warmer months...we saw snow for the first time. It snowed before Opening Day, in fact.

Meanwhile in New York, their third baseman, Dick Howser, broke his arm. The Yankees had sent a scout to watch me. I was supposed to stay with the Dodgers for the whole year, but the Yankees needed me back to play third base. A new deal was struck with the Dodgers, and I was on my way back to the big leagues. The Yankees sent John Miller, a guy who homered in his first Major League at bat in 1966, back to the Dodgers in exchange for me.

In total, I played 84 games in the Dodgers' organization for the Spokane Indians. I held my own defensively as the third baseman there, thanks, of course, to Tommy Hutton's glove. I also hit very well. In those 84 games, I batted .343 and hit six homers. I would never play in the minor leagues again.

I met the Yankees on July 19, 1967 in Cleveland and was immediately starting at third. I was once again batting second in the lineup right in front of Mickey Mantle. I went 1 for 4 that first game back. The next day, facing the hard-throwing lefty Sam McDowell, I had another hit.

The life of a baseball player calls for him to have to move

quickly when he gets called to a new team. A lot falls on his family to handle moving, and all of the other things that life entails. Linda made all of the moving arrangements at home and soon flew to New York where we'd be living in the Bronx at the Concourse Plaza Hotel. Her first interaction with New York wasn't the best. As we unpacked our suitcases and brought them up to our apartment, we had a "Welcome to the Bronx" moment—someone stole two of our suitcases. As I recall, it was mostly Linda's stuff.

I had a lime green 1967 Mercury Cougar at the time. We had a car service drive the car from Los Angeles out to us in New York. They got the car to us quickly, but it never ran great after that. I imagine whoever drove the car coast to coast had some fun at the car's expense. And mine!

Playing third base for the Yankees was a disaster for me. Instead of throwing the ball across the diamond to the young and athletic Tommy Hutton who could catch everything, I had to throw the ball to Mickey Mantle at first base. Every throw had to be right on the money because Mickey couldn't move all that well. And that was something I just couldn't do consistently or all that well. The fans didn't appreciate my erratic play. They were used to seeing Clete Boyer at third who was among the best to ever field the position. It was a big drop off from Boyer to Roy White.

At Yankee Stadium, third base is situated very close to the fans. I heard the catcalls and the boos. I ended up playing only 17 games at third base. In that time, I made eight errors. The bad fielding also affected my hitting. In one game, on July 26, against the Minnesota Twins, in the second game of a doubleheader, and in a game that itself went 18 innings, I went hitless in eight at bats. They soon moved me off of third base and back to the outfield where I played sporadically for the rest of the season.

Overall, in 1967, I played in just 70 games for the Yankees and had a batting average for the season of .224 with two home runs and just 18 runs batted in.

My big league career to that point wasn't much to brag about. For two seasons, I didn't hit well. I also didn't have a position. They tried me at each outfield position, second base, and third base. As the 1967 season ended, I was beginning to wonder what my future held.

Chapter 5
Putting It All Together
1968-1970

HEADING TO SPRING TRAINING, for the 1968 season, I did not know where I was at. I didn't know much about where my career was going, what position I would be playing, or even if I would stay with the Major League club. Well, I knew one thing, the Yankees would be crazy to play me at third base. I was pretty certain that wouldn't be happening.

At the start of camp, Ralph Houk called me into his office. He told me that he had figured it all out. He told me that I shouldn't worry about playing infield any longer, that I was going to be an outfielder exclusively. That spring, that's all I worked on, becoming the best outfielder I could be.

The best tip I ever received came from Tom Tresh that spring. He said, "Roy, when you go after a fly ball, pretend like you are going to catch an egg. That will keep you relaxed." He also advised me to use only one hand, rather than two, the way we were taught as kids. That relaxed feeling was something I worked on all spring. I learned it and it benefited me greatly throughout my career.

I had a decent spring and made the team as the fourth or fifth outfielder. That's not great, but I was happy just to be on the big league roster. I was heading north, for the second time in my career, with the Yankees.

***

We opened the 1968 season in New York. I appeared in four games in that series, each as a pinch hitter. I had one hit, a single off Jim Perry, that came on Opening Day.

We then went on the road for our first away series. The good news was that the trip was to Los Angeles to play the Angels. I was very excited to get home and see my wife Linda and our new baby, my daughter Loreena who had been born while I was in Spring Training. Back then, players didn't leave to be with their wives and families when their children were born. The way the teams saw it, a player's first loyalty was to them.

Linda met me at the airport, but without the baby who was left at the apartment with my mother-in-law. When we finally arrived, I got to see my daughter for the first time. The next night, to give Linda some needed rest, I stayed up with Loreena who was crying most of the night. I was glad to do this, and I knew it wouldn't matter much to my baseball career. I knew I wouldn't be playing the next day; I was a reserve player after all.

The next day, tired, but content, I drove out to the stadium. I soon found out that I was starting in right field because Joe Pepitone had broken his arm.

In my first at bat, I singled to center. In my next at bat, I dropped a bunt single down the third base line. In my third at bat, I homered.

The next day, I was starting again in right field. I had two more hits including a double.

And that's how it all started.

After staying up all night with Loreena, I was put in the lineup and was a regular part of the Yankees lineup for the next twelve years. In a way, my daughter helped make me an everyday Major Leaguer.

I wasn't the starting left fielder yet, though. That would come later. At first, I played a lot of right field, but I was then moved to center. I spent most of the month of May as the Yankees' starting centerfielder. DiMaggio to Mantle to White, once again!

On May 22, Ralph Houk moved me to left field because Joe Pepitone was returning. Ralph said that left field would be a great place for me because of the vastness of that area in our home park. Playing left field in Yankee Stadium was like playing in center in any other park. There was that much room to cover. The Yankees needed a player that could cover a lot of ground. That player, as it turned out, was me. I always felt that centerfield was an easier position to play because the ball comes right at you and there are no angles to learn how to play. As a centerfielder, you also have outfielders on either side of you, but left field was my new home.

Moving to left field provided an additional challenge besides the new angles balls would take off the bat and the fact that the space was so expansive. In Yankee Stadium, left field was the sun field. This is something every player who comes to New York knows about Yankee Stadium during day games. The sun is a killer. By 3:00 p.m., the sun was right over the third deck and it shined right into the eyes of the left fielder. I knew that in those Saturday and Sunday day games (which back then, most of the weekend games were), there would be a chance that I would lose the ball in the sun. Learning to play the Yankee Stadium sun is a huge task and was one I worked diligently to master.

Some players never master the Yankee Stadium sun. In fact, I remembered Norm Siebern costing the Yankees a World Series game in 1958 against the Braves because he lost at least two fly balls in the sun. I didn't want that to ever happen to me.

I overcame this challenge partly through prayer and hoping for overcast days.

During that season Ralph Houk also made me the clean-up hitter for the Yankees. Mickey Mantle, who batted third, wasn't getting any good pitches to hit, so they moved me to fourth, "clean-up," to hit behind Mantle and protect him. That was the next big step in my career. I was basically the Yankees' clean-up hitter (in the first years sharing the spot with Joe Pepitone) from that point through the 1972 season. The next player to hold that position in the batting order for that long wouldn't come for a number of years after. His name was Reggie Jackson.

There was a particularly memorable day for me in July

at Cleveland. We were up against Stan Williams, a longtime big league pitcher and a former Yankee. In that game, I had two hits off him. My first time up, I doubled. Then I singled. In my third at bat, I worked the count to 3-0 and that's when Stan drilled me with the next pitch right into my hip. Williams threw what they called a "heavy ball." It was one of the most painful times I was ever hit. Later on the bench I sat next to Mickey Mantle who was laughing. He said, "I could have told you old Stan was going to get you. He didn't like that you had two hits off him. He had to pay you back." It seems that Williams, known as "the big hurt," kept a list of all the guys he needed to hit with a pitch, mostly guys who homered off of him. The rumor was that he was always trying to get even with Hank Aaron, but he could never hit him. The rumor also said that he even tried to throw a pick-off throw to first base when Aaron was there, but he missed him there too.

The 1968 season was a tough one in which to hit. It became known as "The Year of the Pitcher." Only one player in the entire American League hit higher than .300, Carl Yastrzemski who batted .301. The second-best hitter in the league was Danny Cater who hit .290. Quite simply, the pitchers just dominated. Denny McLain of the Tigers won 31 games. My teammate Mel Stottlemyre was tied for third in the league with 21 wins. Five pitchers, in the American League alone, had Earned Run Averages under 2.00 for the season.

For the season, I batted .267 which was just out of the top ten of all batters in the league. I found myself among the league leaders in games played (159, 3rd), runs (89, 3rd), hits (154, 6th), triples (7, 7th), walks (73, 8th), stolen bases (20, 10th), and total bases (239, 10th). That wasn't bad for a player who was just happy to go north with the team out of Spring Training. Because of my success, I received consideration for the MVP and finished 12th overall in the voting.

As I look back, 1968 was the end of a big era in Yankees history. As I was slowly establishing myself as a Major League ballplayer, the great Yankees of my youth were slowly being traded away or retiring. After the 1966 season, Roger Maris was traded to the St. Louis Cardinals. In August 1967, Elston

Howard was traded to the Red Sox. Bobby Richardson retired after the 1966 season. Whitey Ford retired during the 1967 season. And the 1968 season proved to be the last one for Mickey Mantle. An era had passed. The Yankees were no longer a great team. And the great players who had been on the championship teams were now gone.

Right as the season ended, I was assigned to another team, The United States Army Reserves. At the time, in order not to lose two years of our playing careers, many baseball players went into the reserves. It was a way to not get drafted. Not all the players did this, of course, and for some, they lost significant time. Bobby Murcer, for one, lost two years of his career after being drafted. I believe he spent much of his military service playing baseball, but still, it wasn't the Major Leagues. Another player, Rich Beck, with whom I share my Topps rookie card, was drafted on the day before his twenty-sixth birthday. A man was eligible for the draft only until he was twenty-six. For Beck, he was drafted on the very last day of his eligibility. His service time was two years, of course. While in the Army, he hurt his arm. Just before being drafted, Beck had pitched three games for the Yankees in 1965 including a complete game shutout. After his time in the military, he never made it back to the Major Leagues. For my assignment, I had to complete six months of active duty including, of course, at the start, Basic Training. I went right in after the season ended in October. I was stationed at Fort Dix in New Jersey. This was the first off-season that I did not return to California.

Basic Training was tough. They certainly did not take it easy on me because I was a ballplayer, a Yankee, or even a guy who was considered for the Most Valuable Player Award. They trained us hard. What you see of Basic Training in the movies or on TV is often pretty accurate. The days were long. We exercised. We ran. We drilled.

If the difficult training didn't make me miss my home in Los Angeles, the cold New Jersey winter certainly did. The winter of 1968 to 1969 was one of the coldest on record. And the snow came and came. A year previous, the snow of Spokane was a fun novelty—something new, different, and wonderful. It wasn't any of those things any longer. In February, there was a nor'easter that lasted for three days and dumped almost two feet of snow on New York City paralyzing the region.

I remember just being cold. On our first overnight assignment, we went camping on a cold night. Our leader advised us to get out of our clothes to stay warmer in our sleeping bags as we slept. I took the advice and woke up freezing and wishing I had kept my clothes on.

When Spring Training arrived, I was able to join the team for some weekends only. As far as the Army saw it, I worked for them. They were my first priority. I flew out of New Jersey on Friday nights, trained with the Yankees in Florida during the weekend, returned to the base on Sunday, and then served the United States Army during the week.

By this time, my Basic Training over. I was assigned as a company clerk. In that role, they didn't work me too hard. We sat around talking on most days. I would have rather been in Florida with the team, but I also realized how fortunate I was. This was especially true when veterans from Vietnam returned home and shared stories with us about combat, injuries, and the horrors of war.

Once the 1969 season started, I still had to still fulfill my obligation to Uncle Sam. Six months of active duty was six months. The United States Army was going to make sure they got every day out of me. I understood and respected this, but it wasn't always easy. Throughout the season, I had to miss games because of Army Reserve meetings and training that took place on some weekends. I recall once flying out to California with the Yankees for a west coast trip that began in Los Angeles. After playing against the Angels, I had to fly home to serve at the reserve unit in downtown New York City. At the end of that weekend, I had to then fly all the way back to California to meet the team in Oakland.

The 1969 Yankees, unfortunately, were still not very good. After going 11-10 in April, we had losing records in May and June and July.

Mickey Mantle had announced his retirement in March

of 1969. On June 8, the Yankees celebrated Mantle's career with Mickey Mantle Day. The stadium was packed. I remember being in awe of the packed stadium and the reverence in which Mantle was held. He came into the locker room before the game and talked with us. It was a special day and one that was truly the end of an era.

On that day, Mickey Mantle's uniform number 7 was retired. It was only the fourth number the Yankees ever retired as Mantle joined Lou Gehrig (#4), Babe Ruth (#3), and Joe DiMaggio (#5). Now no one would ever wear uniform #7 again. In 1969, the player who had the one uniform number in between all of those legends, #6, was me.

Today, the Yankees retire many uniform numbers. There have been a host of players who have received that honor. Back when I first played, that honor was reserved only for the truly legendary players, the greatest of the greats.

During that 1969 season, one very special honor for me was that I made the American League All-Star team. In those days, the starters were picked by the players in the league and the manager, in this case Mayo Smith of the Tigers, picked the reserves. I was honored to be chosen for the team by Mayo Smith. I had enjoyed a very successful first half of the season that year batting .313 with 46 runs batted in. The only other All-Star to come from the Yankees that year was Mel Stottlemyre who was the starting pitcher for the A.L. squad.

The All-Star Game was played in Washington DC. One of the big thrills we had was going to the White House and meeting President Nixon who congratulated each of us with a handshake. On that trip, I roomed with Rod Carew. That's how we became friends. I always looked forward to playing against the Minnesota Twins because Horace Clarke and I would meet Rod Carew and Tony Oliva after the games to hang out, usually at a nice restaurant, and talk baseball.

The 1969 All-Star game was filled with some of baseball's greatest stars. There were a host of future Hall of Famers on both teams. In the American League, we had Rod Carew, Tony Oliva, Reggie Jackson, Carl Yastrzemski, Harmon Killebrew, Brooks Robinson, and Frank Robinson. The National League team had Hank Aaron, Roberto Clemente, Willie Mays, Ernie Banks, Johnny Bench, Tony Perez, Willie McCovey, Phil Niekro, Steve Carlton, Tom Seaver, Bob Gibson, Juan Marichal, and Ron Santo. What a collection of talent!

In the All-Star game, I pinch hit in the ninth inning against Phil Niekro who in his career eventually won over 300 games. Niekro was a knuckleball pitcher. I remember battling him pretty well. The first five pitches he threw were knuckleballs. A few were balls and I fouled off a couple of others. I battled him pitch-for-pitch, but I was down to my final strike. The last thing I ever expected him to throw was a fastball right down the middle, but he did. I took it, and it was strike three.

As I look back at that 1969 season, I realize that those army meetings and the travel cut into my routine. Baseball is a game of routines and the disruptions definitely hurt my production. In 1968, the "Year of the Pitcher," I hit 17 home runs. In 1969, I connected for only seven. Overall, I batted .290, my best year to date in that regard, but I wonder if I could have batted .300 with just a little more consistency. I played in only 130 games in 1969. That was the fewest number of games I played in through the entirety of my career as a starting player—up through the 1977 season. In the period from 1968 through the 1973 season, I averaged 157 games played in every season except that 1969 season.

Over time, I learned that other players who owed the Reserves some military time had more lenient military commanders. Some of these commanders allowed the ballplayers to make their military time on days the team had off. These players were not flying back-and-forth coast to coast to serve their military obligations and also play Major League Baseball. I certainly did not have that good fortune at that time.

I remember another time when the Yankees were playing the Detroit Tigers. I began the day at the base in New York City. The Yankees played a doubleheader that day. I missed the first game completely. My obligation ended at 4:00 p.m., so I hopped on an uptown train and rushed to the ballpark and played in the second game. I also missed some games that year because I had to report to Camp Drum way up in New

York State at the Canadian border. Bud Harrelson of the Mets and Thurman Munson, my future teammate with the Yankees, were also there. We served, but it was typical Army Reserve stuff—"hurry up and wait." We didn't do much except wait to get back to playing baseball.

My military career actually ended during the U.S. Postal Strike that took place between March 18 and March 25, 1970. For this strike, we were called into active duty. I had to leave Spring Training to go to New York and serve. During this brief period, I drove into New York City each day from my home in West Paterson, New Jersey. Then we waited in the barracks for an assignment. None came. But, because this was considered active duty, it ended my military obligation.

With no more military service in 1970, I ended up playing in every single game. The only other player to play in every game that year was Sandy Alomar of the California Angels. He would one day be my teammate on the Yankees.

I made a big change in my approach to the game for the 1970 season. Prior to that season, I wore glasses on the field. It's a challenge playing baseball in glasses. As you exercise, the lenses can tend to fog up. On humid days at the plate, this would also happen. It wasn't easy to hit the great pitchers in the league with perfect eyesight. Hitting against them with glasses that were foggy, hazy, or, during a rainy game, sprinkled with raindrops was an even bigger challenge.

Playing the outfield in glasses also caused problems. Playing in the direct sun was especially difficult. We had these sunglasses that we could flip down when trying to catch a fly ball. Because of my regular glasses, I had to wear a bigger pair that went over my glasses. This added an awkward element to the whole process. Playing in the rain could be a nightmare. I once cost Mel Stottlemyre a shutout because I misjudged a fly ball in the rain and dropped it.

To eliminate all of those issues and problems, I began wearing contact lenses for the 1970 season. I wore them for the rest of my playing days.

The change seemed to work. For the first half of the season, I was hitting everything in sight. After the game on June

17, my batting average was at an all-time personal high of .360. For a period, I was leading the league in hitting. Because of this, I was voted into my second All-Star game, this time by the players. This was a huge honor.

I was going to be one of the starting players that year, but a circumstance just before the game ruined that dream. During batting practice, a photographer from *The Sporting News* approached me and asked me to go down the left field line for a photo shoot. Because of my success, I was going to be on the cover of the weekly newspaper known to many as the "Bible of Baseball." There wasn't a more important magazine or newspaper in the sport than *The Sporting News*. That issue came out on August 22, 1970. I am pictured in my right-hand-ed batting stance. I'm choking up on the bat slightly.

As the photo shoot was taking place, the feared slugger Dick Allen was taking batting practice. He hit a rocket right at me. It might have taken a bounce first, I actually don't recall, but it hit me hard in the arm forcing me to see the trainer. The American League manager, Earl Weaver, advised me to take care of the arm. Because of this, I did not get my chance to start. Weaver indicated that he would find a place for me to pinch hit.

That 1970 mid-summer classic was also filled with some all-time greats of the game. The American League team in-cluded future Hall of Famers Rod Carew, Luis Aparacio, Carl Yastrzemski, Frank Robinson, Brooks Robinson, Tony Oliva, Harmon Killebrew, Jim Palmer, and Jim "Catfish" Hunter, who, in a few years would be my teammate and help the Yankees finally get back to the World Series. The National League team included Hank Aaron, Willie Mays, Willie McCovey, Roberto Clemente, Joe Morgan. Tony Perez, Johnny Bench, Tom Seaver, Bob Gibson, Hoyt Wilhelm, and Gaylord Perry. Joe Torre, the future Yankees manager, and a Hall of Famer himself was also a player on that National League team. Three Yankees made the team that year, Mel Stottlemyre, Fritz Peterson, and me.

I watched the game from the sidelines in the dugout wish-ing I could be part of the action. Inning after inning I sat. Earl Weaver just didn't get me into the game. It looked like the

American League was going to win the game as they had a 4-1 lead heading into the bottom of the 9th inning, but the N.L. scored three times—all off current or future Yankees pitchers (Hunter, Peterson, and Stottlemyre) and the game went into extra innings where the game remained tied inning after inning.

After we batted and failed to score in the 12th inning, Earl Weaver alerted me that my opportunity to bat was going to come in the top of the thirteenth inning. But it wasn't to be. Instead, history took over.

In one of baseball's most famous plays, with two outs in the bottom of the 12th inning, the National League staged a rally. Pete Rose singled. Billy Grabarkewitz followed with a single of his own. And then Jim Hickman came up and also singled. Pete Rose, who had been on second base, never stopped running and came home at the exact moment that the ball arrived, and he crashed into our catcher Ray Fosse and scored the game-winning run. This was hard-nosed old-fashioned baseball, and today it would be frowned upon, but in 1970, that was the way the game was played. Fosse suffered from a separated shoulder, but I don't recall any of the players feeling that it was a dirty play. The same types of collisions happened all the time at home plate and around the bag at second base often. Baseball could be, and was, a rough sport.

After the All-Star break, I fell into a rut and saw my average drop and drop and drop. It is difficult to play in every single game over the course of a 162 game season. This involved playing in both ends of doubleheaders. Days off were rare. We also had plenty of day games in the hot sun.

We'd arrive at the park, usually three or four hours before game time. There was a lot of work to do that the fans didn't see. There were drills, outfield practice as part of the pre-game routine, and meetings to discuss the other players and pitchers, where to play them, and what to look for.

I must have been somewhat run down as the season wore on because the hits just stopped coming. My average dropped to a season low of .289 on August 23. That's not a bad batting average, but it was a far cry from the .360 I was hitting earlier.

In late August, I hit the first grand slam of my career. It came against future Hall of Famer Bert Blyleven of the Twins.

At that point, good fortune found me again. I hit well the rest of the way and ended at .296 which would be my career high. I also slugged 22 home runs, also a season high for my career.

With Mantle, Maris, Howard, and Ford departed, in a sense a new era had dawned for the Yankees. In place of the superstars were players like me, up-and-comers. Bobby Murcer, who many felt would one day be the next Mickey Mantle was another. The constant who would play second base was Horace Clarke. And on the mound, we had Mel Stottlemyre.

These three players were all very good ballplayers and people. Bobby and I played together for years and batted behind each other in the lineup. Our skills complemented each other. Horace Clarke and I were roommates in Spring Training in 1963. We really hit it off because we had a lot in common. We both loved jazz music. I brought my portable record player to Spring Training and then during the season also carried it along when we were on the road. We loved listening to Cal Tjader who played Latin Jazz. His expertise was the vibraphone. Clarke learned how to play that instrument and after his playing career he had his own band. He was quite good. We also loved Horace Silver, Cannonball Adderley, and Miles Davis.

Mel Stottlemyre was, of course, a pitcher. As such, we had different routines. The pitchers and the everyday players shared a clubhouse and were teammates, and many times friends, but on a baseball team, we often live in different universes.

In 1970, as a team, we performed well. We won 93 games and finished in second place to the Orioles. After so many down years, including that last place finish in 1966, Fritz Peterson decided we should celebrate finishing second with champagne and all of that in the locker room after the season's final game. Finishing in second place was a big step forward for us and we felt it was a signal that we had finally turned the corner. But, with the Yankees' long tradition of greatness, our exploits were frowned upon by some of the writers. "Imagine that," they said, "The great New York Yankees celebrating for finishing in second place."

One reason we took a big step forward was the addition of another player who would be central to the Yankees' success going forward. He was the player who won the 1970 Rookie of the Year Award, a great new player who brought a winning attitude with him, our catcher, and future Captain, Thurman Munson. His presence helped the Yankees eventually become champions. He and I were the only players to remain with the club from that 1970 season through the World Series years.

Of course, I got to know Thurman very well. Our lockers were right next to each other.

We both felt that greatness was just ahead…

Chapter 6
The Final CBS Years
1971-1972

GREATNESS DIDN'T COME AS quickly as we had suspected or hoped. In fact, in a way we peaked in 1970 and were about to face a five-year period of mediocrity with some years slightly better than the next, but there were no championships, and for the most part, there was no glory on the horizon. It was a slow climb to get the Yankees back to the World Series. What first seemed so close in 1970 seemed to get further and further away especially as the years rolled on. In a way, I lump the seasons after 1970, but before 1976, together. We played okay baseball. We were good, sometimes, but we were never great, and we didn't threaten anyone.

Just before this time, New York, of course, did have a World Championship baseball team. That was in 1969, only it wasn't us, it was the Mets. The Miracle Mets and their amazing success made it seem like anything could happen. I think that was one reason we thought that after that 1970 season, we'd immediately be good again as well. If the Mets could reach the World Series, and win it, anything was possible.

The New York Mets entered the National League in 1962 and immediately became a team known for losing. That first year, they set a record for losses in a season. They lost 120 games that year. For their first seven seasons, from 1962 through 1968, the Mets never finished a season higher than ninth place in the ten team league. Then, in 1969, they won it all.

The Yankees in the 1960s also hit rock bottom. After

reaching (and losing) the 1964 World Series, the Yankees finished in fifth place in 1965. The 1966 season saw us finish in last place. In 1967, we weren't much better, finishing in ninth place out of ten teams. But then we started to get better. We finished in fifth place in 1968 and 1969 before the second place finish in 1970. But then, we fell back again.

In some ways it got monotonous. I wasn't playing for a job any longer. I was an established player, considered by many as a star. For this group of Yankees teams, the stars were Bobby Murcer, Thurman Munson, and me. Bobby Murcer was the biggest star of the three of us. He was an American League All-Star in every season from 1971 through 1974. He'd routinely hit .300 and blast 20 to 30 homers a year. Bobby though, as I'll share, was traded to the San Francisco Giants after the 1974 season in a move that surprised and shocked us all. The other star, who played with me through this whole period, was Thurman Munson. Only tragedy prohibited Thurman from being the only player, along with me, to be a Yankee for the entire decade of the 1970s.

At first glance, I remember the start of this period as one that did not bring us even close to the postseason. In 1971, 1972, and 1973, for three consecutive years, we finished in fourth place. We had winning records in 1971 (82-80) and 1972 (79-76), and were slightly under .500 in 1973 (80-82). Lots of the same. Good. Not great.

I signed with the Yankees, a team with a long history of winning, a winning tradition that lasted decades, and now I was a Yankee, and I wondered if I'd ever be part of a winner. I wondered what winning felt like in New York. I wondered if the champagne shower that we celebrated second place with in 1970 was the closest I'd ever come to playing on a true winner.

This was a period where a host of former stars came to play in pinstripes. Boy did we see our share of big names coming in. Unfortunately, most of these new teammates were well past their primes. The Yankees in those years had guys like Ron Swoboda, who had been a hero with the 1969 Miracle Mets and Curt Blefary who had won the Rookie of the Year with the Baltimore Orioles in 1965. Swoboda hit just .235 as a Yankee over three seasons. Blefary hit just .210. Lindy McDaniel, respected by all as a very good pitcher and a great person, was our closer for a number of years. He had been an All-Star with the Cardinals in 1960, a long time previous.

Other stars who passed through, some who played well enough, but none who ultimately helped us win enough to reach the postseason, were Felipe Alou, Johnny Callison, Matty Alou, Jim Ray Hart, Mike Hegan, and Sudden Sam McDowell.

One player came to us from the Mexican League and was, for a time, one of the most exciting players on the Yankees. For a period, he took New York by storm. His name was Celerino Sanchez, a dynamic third baseman whose star shined brightly, but only for a brief period.

Until the 1974 season, it seemed to be a lot of the same, year-after-year, but, in retrospect, it wasn't at all.

The 1972 season brought with it Major League Baseball's first player's strike.

And, in 1973, everything changed for the Yankees because CBS, who had owned the team through all those lean years, sold the team to a dynamic owner named George Steinbrenner. Once Steinbrenner and his General Manager Gabe Paul took over the club, things started to change, and change quickly. When George Steinbrenner first took over the team, he stated that he was going to be a hands-off owner. That certainly was not the case. At all.

And, all of a sudden there were trades and more trades. These were not like the previous ones where aging stars were brought in. Gabe Paul seemed like a genius to us as many of the players he acquired weren't stars yet, but a host of them soon would be. He found the diamonds who would soon be polished and who would form the foundation for the Yankees' World Series teams in 1976, 1977, and 1978.

In those years right after George Steinbrenner bought the team, some of the best players I ever played with, and some who became life-long friends, joined the Yankees. These players, the ones who brought us back, finally, to the team's winning tradition included Chris Chambliss, Lou Piniella,

Mickey Rivers, Ed Figueroa, Willie Randolph, and Bucky Dent.

And then there was free agency with George Steinbrenner right at the center of it all. The first big catch we had was Jim "Catfish" Hunter in 1975. Reggie Jackson came in 1977. Rich "Goose" Gossage in 1978. Not all the free agent signings worked out over the long term. Don Gullet and Andy Messersmith were two very good pitchers who the Yankees signed, but both were soon injured.

A new era was dawning, one that would be focused on winning, not losing; success, not mediocrity.

A lot was going on, both on the field, and off. And I was there, right in the middle of it all, as the only player to be a Yankee for that entire tumultuous decade.

But, before I get ahead of myself, let me take a few steps back.

***

Heading into the 1971 season, we were full of hope. The Yankees, for the first time in six years, had finished higher than fifth place. We felt we were a team on the rise. Mel Stottlemyre, Fritz Peterson, and I had been All-Stars in 1970. Bobby Murcer was fast becoming a star of his own. And we had a young leader who had just won the 1970 Rookie of the Year Award, our catcher, Thurman Munson.

We had a lot of talent on that 1971 team. Also in the starting rotation was Stan Bahnsen, our third best starting pitcher. He had been the Rookie of the Year in 1968. We knew that minor leaguers like Ron Blomberg, a first-round draft pick, were soon going to arrive. And there were steady contributors like second baseman Horace Clarke who, though he never played in an All-Star Game, often played at an All-Star level.

Hopes were high, but the results never came. Our team just never got going. We couldn't beat the better teams in the league. We could hang with them for six or seven innings, and then their better talent would win out. I recall a lot of games where we felt we had the Orioles defeated, but then Frank or Brooks Robinson or Boog Powell would come through and deliver a clutch hit and we'd be on the short end again. The difference between us and the best clubs was that they were just deeper.

It takes a lot of parts to be a top club. We were close, but we weren't there yet.

That season, the three best teams in the American League were the Baltimore Orioles, the Oakland A's, and the Detroit Tigers. We had a losing record against each of those teams. We could defeat or even beat up on the lesser teams, like the Cleveland Indians (who we went 10-8 against) and the Milwaukee Brewers who we defeated in 10 of 12 games that year. We knew we weren't the doormats of the league, but we weren't able to take the next step and defeat the best clubs.

I had been an All-Star in 1970, but, in some ways, my 1971 season was even better. For the season, I batted .292 with 19 home runs and 84 runs batted in. I always prided myself in being able to be a batter who came through in the clutch, and I did just that in 1971 setting the American League Record (one that still stands today, though tied by Bobby Bonilla) for the most sacrifice flies in a season with 17. I also set a record that can never be broken. That year in the outfield, I made no errors. I had a perfect season defensively.

In 1972, there was the Player's Strike. This was a first in professional sports in America. This signaled a watershed moment. We knew that things for us as players, in many ways, would never be the same again.

I remember Marvin Miller who was the head of the player's union coming in and talking to the team in the clubhouse and mentioning things like player's rights, the ability to negotiate, minimum salaries, and things like that which were new to us. People were thinking of the game and our rights as employees as ways in which none of us really ever had before. I was aware of Curt Flood and what he went through during his labor battles. He was a true champion of the players; someone who sacrificed a great deal to get us on the path to winning the rights we eventually gained. But, for the most part, most of us didn't pay too much attention to that. We did as the teams told us. We just played baseball and were glad to be big leaguers. When Curt Flood was challenging baseball's

Reserve Clause, I was just starting to establish my career. I was in no position, even if that had been in my personality, to rock the boat.

Before free agency and agents and all of that, we would basically just get a contract in the mail. If we didn't like the amount, we might write in what we thought we should earn, but the team didn't have to give that to us. There wasn't really any negotiation. The teams had us. They could pay us what they wanted. If we didn't like it, we could go home. By the early 1970s, I was living in New York year-round so I would meet Lee McPhail, the General Manager, face-to-face and we'd "negotiate." At the end of the day, if I got half of what I asked for, I felt I did well. As players, we didn't talk about our salaries very much, if at all. I know that most of the players felt as I did. In a large part, although we would have loved to make more money, we were just happy to be big league baseball players. This system was the one baseball had operated under for decades. The teams, through the Reserve Clause, which bound us to the teams we were on, held all the power.

Over time, I started keeping my own stats to show my value and I would use that information in the negotiations. The Yankees didn't always value the information I brought to the table. But, in the end, I think it helped, at least a little.

It's important to note that none of us was rich. Baseball didn't pay huge salaries to the players back then. Some of the stars, maybe Mickey Mantle or Willie Mays, made higher salaries, but the other players, guys like me, didn't make a whole lot of money.

In those years, in order to make a living because we didn't get paid in the off-season, I had winter jobs. One year I worked for Potamkin Cadillac in Manhattan selling cars. I sold one car that year. Another year I worked for CBS doing spots sales. I don't remember being all that successful in that area either. I mostly remember working in BlackRock in the city and spending a lot of time at Toots Shor's eating lunches with prospective clients. Toots Shor's was a big time place for some of the city's biggest names. Joe DiMaggio would sometimes be there. Howard Cosell as well. I was a ballplayer, none of this was what I wanted to be doing with my time. One winter, before I moved to New York full time, I worked at the Sears Roebuck warehouse in Los Angeles. I did stock work and also some tasks like drilling the finer holes in bowling balls and putting sewing machines into their furniture cases. When he was with the Yankees, I saw Cecil Fielder and he said that his father had worked with me all those years previously at the Sears warehouse.

Once I became an established big leaguer, my pay increased, and I didn't have to find as many opportunities to work in the off season. My initial salary in 1966 was $7,000, the Major League minimum. My salary didn't rise quickly from that point. In 1967, it was about $9,000. In 1968, it was increased to $12.000., But remember, we did not get paid in the winter. By the early 1970s, my salary had risen into the $40,000-$50,000 range.

Rather than working part time jobs, in the 1970s, I was paid to do appearances. I also sometimes found myself with some unique opportunities. In 1975, I actually had the chance to star in a Hollywood movie titled *The Premonition*. It was what one might call a psychological thriller. I played a character named Dr. Larabee. The movie wasn't a big hit, but it was fun seeing and being part of the entertainment industry. For a guy who grew up in California, with Hollywood not far from home, it added a special thrill, but it didn't add up to more money. I was actually a small investor in the movie. I had jokingly said to the director, "I'd like a role." And he gave me one. I also invested and acted in a second movie called *Rebel* with Sylvester Stallone before he became famous for the *Rocky* movies. In fact, I didn't even get to meet him because he had already filmed his parts. I didn't make any money from the movies, but these were great experiences.

When the 1972 players' strike came, most of us were nervous. We weren't rich. We needed our baseball salaries to make ends meet. If we were going to miss two or three months, we were going to face some real financial hardships. If there were no games, we wouldn't get paid, of course. We really counted on playing and making our living.

The strike began on April 1, 1972, just before Opening Day. We had already completed Spring Training and the season was all set to go—and then nothing. Most of the players were very much in favor of this action, across the team and across the league. We even received support from professional players in other sports.

Of course, we were athletes and we needed to be ready to play games the moment the strike ended. To stay in shape, I remember heading into the Bronx and working out with some of my teammates on the baseball fields at Macombs Dam Park next to the stadium. A few of us were there including Gene Michael, Horace Clarke, Ron Blomberg, and Jerry Kenney. The coaches couldn't work with us, so we put ourselves through various drills.

The strike didn't last long and was settled on April 13. The players won a few concessions. A half-million dollars was added to our pension fund, and we won the right to have salary arbitration. Things moved quickly after that. The owners wanted us playing, and since the missed games wouldn't be made up, we wanted to get playing as quickly as possible to get paid. We played our first game of the 1972 season on Sunday, April 16. All in all, we only missed about a week. I was greatly relieved when the strike was over, and we could play ball again.

Maybe it was the delay brought on by the strike, or maybe it was something else, but the 1972 season started very poorly for me. By the end of April, I was hitting only .205. I didn't hit my first home run until the last day of April. I also wasn't driving in runs.

In May, I started to get on track, but my best month was June. As the weather warmed up, so did I. I hit over .300 that month. I wasn't able to sustain this though and ended with a solid but disappointing year batting .270 with 10 home runs. One stat that was overlooked back then was walks. I ended tied with Dick Allen for the league lead in walks in 1972 with 99. I knew my job was to get on base and I did. For the 1972 season, I ended fourth in the American League in On-Base Percentage. Again, back then people didn't look at statistics like that. They focused mostly on batting average, home runs, and runs batted in. My teammates, though, knew that I was doing my job.

For the Yankees, with games missed because of the strike, our season was 155 games. I played in every single one of them. I would have been the league leader in games played, but due to the way the schedule worked out, the Detroit Tigers played one more game than us. Eddie Brinkman, the Tigers' shortstop, played in all 156 games of his team's schedule to lead the league. Sandy Alomar of California also played in 155 games.

The 1972 Yankees finished with a good record (79-76). We were better than the bad teams, but we still finished in fourth place in the six team American League East. The clear star of our team, by then, was Bobby Murcer and 1972 was one of his best years. He hit .292 with 33 home runs. In some ways, he was starting to remind us of Mickey Mantle. That year we also added Sparky Lyle who pitched great for us out of the bullpen.

The best part of the 1972 season though didn't happen on the field. On September 30, my son Reade was born. I was at the ballpark getting ready for the game. Ralph Houk called me into his office and told me that my wife was in labor and that I had permission to leave the stadium to be with her. And, while Reade didn't help me with a hot streak since the 1972 season was just about over when he arrived, he would provide a special spark later in my career in a significant way.

Chapter 7
The First Years with George Steinbrenner
1973-1975

THE 1973 SEASON BROUGHT with it the arrival of George M. Steinbrenner III. Although it would take a few years for us to get to the World Series, that was the true turning point. We almost knew this from the start. When CBS owned the Yankees, they hadn't been willing to spend the necessary money to get enough quality players or improve the farm system. George was ready to lay it all out there to bring the Yankees back. Almost immediately, deals were made, and the Yankees started changing.

It must be noted, though, that two of the most important pieces to the championship puzzle were both acquired in 1972, one player before the season, and one after. The great Sparky Lyle, a relief pitcher who would anchor our staff, becoming a bastion of reliability, and who would close out game after game (and who would win the 1977 American League Cy Young Award) was acquired in March, right before the 1972 season.

After the 1972 season, the Yankees made a big trade with the Cleveland Indians to get third baseman Graig Nettles, another leader. Nettles would lead the American League in home runs in 1976 and in the early 1980s would be named Captain of the Yankees. So, while George Steinbrenner deserves a lot of credit for bringing the winning back, some foundational pieces were being put into place before his arrival. Those championship players who were already in place included Thurman Munson, Graig Nettles, Sparky Lyle, and me.

When George Steinbrenner first met the team, he talked about making the Yankees great again. He told us that Yankees fans want championships. He promised to deliver this to the fans and to us. Of course, the people who ran the Yankees during the CBS era would have liked the Yankees to win, but they never came into the clubhouse to tell the players that winning was a priority. George Steinbrenner did. This changed the entire dynamic around the team. Steinbrenner set a different tone. I was ready to be on a winner. It had been a long time for the Yankees and their fans, I knew, but it had been a long time for me as well.

One thing that immediately changed with the Yankees was the way we were to look on the field. At about the same time that the Oakland A's were winning the World Series with players with long hair and all sorts of creative mustaches and beards, George Steinbrenner issued a strict dress code for the Yankees. He let us know that there was to be no long hair. Players would not be sporting beards. We were to be well groomed at all times. He wanted us to wear our uniform pants higher to show off the blue socks. He felt that was a more professional look, and George was in the frame of mind that appearances mattered. None of this really impacted me. I didn't have a beard and I never wore my hair long. As for showing my socks, that didn't bother me at all. We all had to follow the grooming rules, but some rules, like showing the blue of the sock, went ignored by many. I felt that none of this kind of stuff mattered. And I believe, even the players who complained about cutting their hair or shaving their beards agreed with me. We felt that we had an owner who wanted to win and that brought with it excitement and anticipation.

The 1973 season for me personally wasn't a great one. My performance reminded me of one of my first years in the minor leagues when everything I hit became an out. I hit into a lot of hard outs. The Law of Averages says that everything should even out in a season, that a player will get soft hits to make up for the hard outs he hits into. I don't think that is the case. Tom Tresh once reasoned that it all might even out for a team, but not for the individual player. Things certainly didn't seem to even out for me in 1973.

Just like in 1972, I got off to a slow start. I hit just .176 in April. Unlike 1972, I never had a great month or two to turn it around. I had a good May, one where I hit about .275, but that didn't get my batting average to respectability.

Baseball is a team sport, but it's also a selfish game. When you're batting, it's just you. There is no one else. It is you against the pitcher. And you want to get your hits. This is the individual part of the team game. This is where our teammates look to us. If we don't produce, we're hurting the team. And if we don't produce, it's very clear. We're all alone out there. When a guy is hitting .200, it's painful. Whenever I slumped or didn't perform, I felt that pressure, from myself and the team. It would be depressing and upsetting to fail to produce. This made us push too hard sometimes and get into bad habits. But the drive to achieve also helped me overcome the slumps to find a way to produce and get the team on the right track.

One flaw in my approach was that my strikeouts went way up that year. Part of this might have been due to a lack of concentration. One thing that is difficult for someone who hasn't played the game to understand is how mentally taxing professional baseball is. It's a grind to get out there and play every game to say nothing of the daily preparation, the travel, playing in front of tens of thousands of fans every day, answering the media, and more. We're also human beings with lives outside the game—families, friends, responsibilities.

I'm not here to make excuses, and I did show up every single day. I played in all 162 games for the Yankees in 1973. This was the first year of the new Designated Hitter rule, but I played all 162 games in the outfield. I was there. I was a loyal and dedicated ballplayer. Further, I played in every inning of every game, including doubleheaders and extra-inning games from the start of the season until August 25. On that day, in Oakland, I batted once in the top of the first inning, struck out, and was replaced by Mike Hegan as the team's left fielder. I then played every inning of every game the rest of the way. I played in 1,467 of the team's 1,476 innings in 1973.

Maybe it wasn't a lack of concentration, but the simple

fact that I must have been exhausted. In 1973, Ralph Houk moved me to the second or third spot in the batting order. I took this responsibility seriously. I was being counted on to get on base and to also drive in runs and that can result in a player altering his swing. Late in games, I waited for pitches that I could drive, hopefully over the right field porch. The big hits in 1973 didn't always come.

Not only did I lead the league in games played (only three other players in the whole league played in every game), but I also led the league in At Bats and Plate Appearances. No one in the league came up to the plate that season more than me. But, my results, a .246 batting average, the lowest of my career, by far, since I became a regular, and the fact that I made an unheard of eight errors in the outfield made me realize that after nine Major League seasons, and as I headed into my thirties, that changes in my game and my conditioning had to be made.

1973 was a strange season for the team. For the first time since 1969, we finished under .500, if just barely at 80-82. We were better than that. We had three players, Bobby Murcer, Graig Nettles, and Thurman Munson, who each hit over 20 home runs, a bigger total back then than it is today. Munson and Murcer also both hit over .300. We also had Ron Blomberg, who played in over 100 games and batted over .320.

On the pitching side, though, it was a different story. Only two pitchers won over ten games, Mel Stottlemyre (16) and rookie Doc Medich (14). Sparky Lyle had a losing record out of the bullpen.

As I noted, 1973 was the year that the Designated Hitter was first adopted. This was supposed to be an experiment for a few years. By no means was this announced as a permanent change that would last forever. But it did. Today no one can even imagine the game, at any level, including with kids, without a DH.

Ron Blomberg was the first player to ever come to bat as a Designated Hitter on Opening Day. For this, he earned a bit of everlasting fame. As my career went on, in the later years, I was employed as a Designated Hitter on occasion. I never really liked being a DH. I always felt that if I played in the field, I would have the opportunity to help the team in a variety of ways. If someone is a DH, the only way he can help the team is to get a hit. Back then, there were also no hitting cages in the stadiums for players to use between at bats. You could go to the clubhouse to swing a bat, but most of the time, it was just being parked on the bench waiting to hit. Sitting around took me out of my regular rhythm. The only time being a DH was a good thing was when we'd play on a cold night in places like Chicago or Minneapolis. In those games, the DH could spend time in the warm locker room instead of freezing in the outfield.

That 1973 season was also strange for two other reasons. First, before the season, in March, when we were all in Spring Training, it came out that two of our pitchers, Fritz Peterson and Mike Kekich traded wives and families—everything. They traded their kids, their homes, and their pets. The reaction among the team was one of disbelief and shock. None of us saw that coming. My wife Linda and I had even been to events with Fritz Peterson and his wife Marilyn who had been a devout Catholic. This came as a big shock, but like other events in the late 1970s, I think it was a bigger story away from the team than on it. We had a job to do—play baseball. The other things were distractions that we didn't pay much attention to.

Fritz Peterson remained with the club all season, but he had a poor year. He had been a top pitcher for us for years averaging 17 wins a year every season from 1969 through 1972. In 1973, he went 8-15. His ERA was the highest it would ever be as a Yankee. He would be traded as part of a franchise changing trade to the Indians the next April. Mike Kekich didn't even last that long. The Yankees shipped him to Cleveland in June of 1973. (Peterson and Kekich wouldn't play together on the Indians. About a month before Cleveland acquired Fritz Peterson, they released Mike Kekich.)

1973 was also the final year that we'd play in the original Yankee Stadium, which opened in 1923. After that year, the building was going to get a complete renovation. Everything would change, from the field to the grandstand to the clubhouse. It was to be a complete remodel. Once the season ended, a lot of the great Yankees history went away in various forms. Once the new stadium opened in 1976, it was beautiful, but it wasn't quite the same.

Even with the losing record, I still think we all felt that the team was on an upward trajectory. Things just felt different. Even with the distractions, we seemed to be moving forward. Even though we'd be playing in a different ballpark in 1974, Shea Stadium, the home of the New York Mets, I was optimistic. But, again, I knew I had to do better.

To remedy the exhaustion or lack of concentration I experienced in 1973, after the season that winter, I got into karate. I was a big fan of Bruce Lee and I saw the physical condition he was in. I also noticed and appreciated the metal concentration at the root of martial arts. I knew this was something I should do in the off-season.

I found a karate dojo in Caldwell, NJ at a place called Koi Kan Karate. Sense Eddie Kaloudis became my trainer. I started training in there two to three times a week. I took this training very seriously. I invested myself in this. I learned the kicks and punches and all of the physical and mental techniques. Some of the deep breathing exercises would soon prove to be beneficial for my baseball career.

I was also free fighting, which was probably not the best idea for a Major League Baseball player—imagine if I sustained an injury! But all went well. I enjoyed this sport and the fitness and mental toughness it gave me. I progressed to green belt level and was even on the cover of *Official Karate* magazine in October of 1975. The title of the article was "Baseball's Roy White Tells How Karate Improved His Game."

***

It was a good thing that I had worked so hard that winter because it was evident early on in Spring Training that 1974 was going to be a very different type of season. For the first time in my career as an established Major Leaguer, we had a new manager, Bill Virdon, and his way of doing things was a lot different than the manager for whom I had been playing since 1966.

When CBS owned the Yankees, they basically left the team alone and let the baseball people run the baseball business. That all changed with George Steinbrenner. He wanted to be involved in all aspects of the game. His hands-on style made being the manager very different than it had been. Throughout most of my career Ralph Houk had been the manager of the Yankees. Ralph was an old-style baseball man. He played on the Yankees as a catcher, backing up Yogi Berra (which means he didn't play much) for years before managing the Yankees from 1961 to 1963. He then became the team's General Manager when Yogi Berra replaced him in the dugout for the 1964 season. During the 1966 last-place finishing season, Houk returned to the field as the manager replacing Johnny Keane.

I enjoyed playing for Ralph Houk because he was fair and honest, and he could be trusted. Ralph Houk respected the players. He trusted us and let us play.

Of all the managers I played for, Ralph Houk was my favorite. He stuck with me through my early lean years. He saw something in me to keep me around long enough to become the player I became. He was truthful in his dealings with me and all the players. If he was going to make a move, he would tell the player to his face. For example, if I was going to be benched for a game, he would sit me down and say, "I want you to see how simple the game is and then you'll play again tomorrow." Here's the key, Ralph Houk always stayed true to his word. Other managers wouldn't always be truthful, even some who would win the World Series. There were times, as I will get into, when a manager might say, "Roy, you're my starter," or "Roy, you'll be playing every game in this series" only to go back on his word almost immediately. For a manager like that, sometimes if you sat for "a game," it became a week. I didn't appreciate that approach. I preferred the way Ralph Houk ran the club.

Ralph Houk was a tough man. He was the boss of the team, there was no doubt about that. You certainly didn't want to cross him. Houk had the respect of the players because of the way he ran the team and because we all knew how strong of a person he was. Houk was a Major in World War II. He served in combat at the Battle of the Bulge and won Army decorations including a Bronze Star, a Silver Star, and a Purple Heart. Ralph respected honesty in his players. He believed in hard work. We learned that you didn't want to cross him or be on his bad side, but we respected that because the only way to get on his bad side would be to be goofing off or doing the wrong thing. Ralph had a good temper too. The good news was, if you hustled and played hard for him, he would be in your corner. That was the way I played ball.

One of Houk's favorite pep talks was, "All we need to do is have you play better than the guy playing your position on the other team." That was great advice, but sometimes that was difficult. I don't know if I could play like Willie Horton of Detroit or Boston's Carl Yastrzemski. I mean, those guys were superstars when I played. But that perspective helped. It made sense and gave us confidence. Because he was hard-nosed, you might not think this, but because he believed in us, Ralph would make us relaxed. He'd also make us laugh. Sometimes he'd even poke fun at himself. I remember one team meeting where he said, "You haven't been playing well, but maybe I haven't been managing so well either."

After the 1973 season, due to the new interference from George Steinbrenner, Ralph Houk resigned. I remember the meeting in the clubhouse at the end of the season when Ralph told the team this news. He said, "No owner is going to tell me how to run a ball club."

Our new manager for 1974 was Bill Virdon. Bill was a strong athletic type who wanted his players to be in the best physical shape possible. The Spring Training camp he ran was unlike any we had ever seen. Virdon was a big proponent of exercise and fitness, and he worked us hard. But it was even harder than that. It was a strenuous camp. A new age was dawning for the Yankees.

Bill Virdon had been an outfielder with the St. Louis Cardinals and the Pittsburgh Pirates—a Gold Glove winning centerfielder known for a strong arm. He was on the 1960

Pirates team that defeated the Yankees in the World Series. It was after that World Series that Ralph Houk took over as the Yankees manager from Casey Stengel. I think Virdon attributed his baseball success to always being in excellent physical shape. Bill also had some success as a manager. He managed the Pittsburgh Pirates in 1972 and 1973. In 1972, he took his team to the fifth game of the National League Championship Series against the Cincinnati Reds before they lost in the bottom of the ninth inning on a wild pitch.

Bill Virdon expected his players to also be in top shape. That Spring Training, he worked us all hard to get us where he felt we needed to be.

Throughout my career, Spring Training had been a time for players to slowly get into shape in the warm Florida sun. We worked. We did what we had to do: exercises, shagging flies, working on cut-offs, and, of course, getting in our batting practice. We did what we had to, but it was at a slower pace, or, at least, not with the rigor and expectations set by Bill Virdon.

For outfield drills, for example, previously, we'd stand in a line, catch the fly ball hit to us, throw it in, and then wait until our turn came up again. We worked on the skill, but it was leisurely and relaxed. There was a lot of chatter between the players as we awaited our turns. Bill did this drill completely differently. Instead of having all the outfielders taking turns, he'd put just two of us out there. He would then hit long fly balls, far away from the players, so far that we would have to sprint to get to the ball. As you were running for the ball hit one way, the other outfielder would be running for the ball hit the other way. Then, just when you caught the ball, threw it in, and quickly returned to your original spot, he'd do it again. Time and time again. The players were running so hard that some were actually getting sick. Ralph Houk may have been a war hero and a soldier, but it was Bill Virdon who ran Spring Training like a boot camp. The days of the long lazy spring warm-ups were over.

There was also another drill, one I liked even less. For this drill, Virdon would bring us in to about 60 feet away and he'd hit rocket ground balls at us. We had to be on our toes. Even as a former infielder who was used to fielding balls that came at me quickly, this drill was a bit harrowing.

After the outfield workouts, we had to run the bases. We ran to first base hard from the batter's box. Then we ran hard from first to third. To end a session, we had to circle the bases. As we ran, Virdon had a stopwatch. If you didn't finish with enough gusto, Virdon would tell you to do it all again. He'd say, "Take another trip around the bases!"

As one might imagine, we also did a lot more hitting too. Practice was to be taken seriously. The players were worked to the maximum. Bill Virdon came on with a seriousness of purpose. He was making sure that the 1974 Yankees were going to be ready for the season.

It was during these drills, as I saw my teammates struggling, that I was so glad that I had started karate. It was through karate that I learned deep breathing. I knew how to handle physical stress without taxing my body as much. This was hard work for all of us, but I was in the best shape of my life and responded better than the guys who didn't come into camp in as good of shape—or not in shape at all. For those guys, Spring Training in 1974 was a killer.

Once the season came, the big change for us was playing at Shea Stadium. That might have been the biggest change and challenge of them all. In a way, it changed everything for the Yankees going forward.

Playing in Shea Stadium was a completely different experience, it wasn't anything close to playing in such a special place like the original Yankee Stadium, but, more than that, the different park impacted us in so many different ways, including changing the way we played baseball and leading to a fan favorite, and friend of mine, being traded.

Playing in Yankee Stadium was something very special. We were in a historic venue, playing on the same field that all the greats had played on—Babe Ruth, Lou Gehrig, Joe DiMaggio, Yogi Berra, on and on. We were part of that lineage with all the greats. There was a lot of history at Yankee Stadium. It was awe inspiring when we'd take a moment to think about it. It was something very special to be part of.

The locker room was spacious. The original lockers were still there—the same ones that the greats had used. There was a lot of majesty and history in the old stadium. A player couldn't help but feel all of that when he first put on the Yankees uniform and every day since. In a way, we had a lot to live up to.

On the playing field, the Yankees prided themselves in having a well-manicured park. The field was well groomed and taken care of. I felt at home out there, in the Yankee Stadium outfield.

Shea Stadium, on the other hand, had the worst outfield I ever played in. This wasn't entirely the fault of the New York Mets, but it still didn't make it enjoyable to play there. Every hit ball was an adventure. Since the Mets and the Yankees were using the same field, almost every day, there was no time for the grounds crew to really take care of the playing surface. There were ruts and divots. Bad hops abounded. It was very difficult to play out there.

One reason Yankee Stadium was so grand was the fact that it was huge. Yankee Stadium actually had the deepest outfield in baseball. This was especially true in left and centerfield areas. As a left fielder in Yankee Stadium, I had to cover a lot of ground. One positive attribute about playing at Shea, was that it was smaller. I had less real estate to have to cover.

Because of the angle of the stadium, the sun also wasn't as much of a problem during the day games at Shea Stadium. It was easier to catch fly balls there. As I think back, if the ball was hit in the air, it was great. It was the bouncing balls, because the ground itself was so uneven, that gave us trouble.

But maybe the worst part about playing in Shea Stadium was that we had to use an auxiliary locker room. This space was smaller and more crowded. We were on top of each other. The locker room is a special place for a team, a place to bond and relax together before and after a game. At Shea we didn't get that luxury. For two years our "home" at the stadium was an uncomfortable area.

At Shea Stadium, we were the home team in 1974 and 1975, but we always felt like a visitor. That wore on us as players. We never felt at home. We were always visitors. It's tough to never feel at home in one's home ballpark.

There was one other drawback to playing at Shea, and it had nothing to do with the stadium itself. It had to do with where it was located. Many of the Yankees players lived in New Jersey in towns scattered across Bergen or Passaic Counties: Norwood, West Paterson, Cresskill, Wyckoff, Tenafly, Ridgewood, and Teaneck. Getting to Yankee Stadium, just on the other side of the George Washington Bridge, was a breeze. Shea was, at least thirty minutes further away—and that was on a good day. To get to Shea, we had to contend with the Triboro Bridge and the Grand Central Parkway. We also didn't have a player's parking area. After the games, we were stuck in the same post-game traffic as all the fans and the other New York City drivers in Queens. I missed the days at Yankee Stadium when I could shower and quickly change after a game and be across the Macombs Dam Bridge and on the Harlem River Drive on my way back to Jersey before most of the fans even exited the Stadium.

All that being said, we had a very good start to the year in 1974. We began the season by winning our first four games, and then played pretty steady ball throughout the season. Like any team, we'd have some short slumps, but we'd bounce back time and again. We were starting to show our resilience. We hadn't been this competitive in years. We were starting to believe that Bill Virdon's training had served us well.

Managers tend to get into routines and run games in a similar manner. Since I had been with Ralph Houk for so long, I could almost always know what he was thinking. Since Bill Virdon was new, this wasn't possible, especially at the start of the season. He also didn't know us as players. As we got to know each other, it was a learning experience. One situation brought about a lot of laughter from some of my teammates— all at my expense.

I wish I could remember all of the specifics, but I recall sitting on the bench near Chris Chambliss and Walt Williams early in the season. We were facing a tough pitcher. I remember it as Nolan Ryan, but whoever it was, was pitching a two-hit shutout or so with a bunch of strikeouts. The game seemed over. None of us thought we'd have to hit. This was a game that was basically over. Jim Mason was walking out to hit. Virdon called him back and yelled, "Roy grab a bat." In that game, no one wanted to hit against Nolan Ryan. He was doing too well. I saw three pitches. They were all strikes. That quickly I had struck out. I was so mad and steaming. I was walking back to the dugout. Chambliss and Williams covered their faces with towels as I walked by because they were laughing so hard. They said, "Roy, you got the guillotine." They laughed about that for days.

Virdon had us in first place in the American League East as late as May 11. It was then that we went into a funk and lost nine of eleven games to fall all the way down to sixth place with a record under .500.

We never got higher than fourth place with a record that hovered around .500 until the end of August when things, all-of-a-sudden, started to click again. Between August 17 and September 4, we went 14-3 and we found ourselves back in first place. When a team gets hot late in the season, they tend to believe that it's because the breaks are finally going their way. It seemed like anything was possible. We were rolling and a pennant seemed possible. As players start to believe, they also begin to perform better.

By September 12, we had a record of 78-66 and were 2.5 games ahead of the second place Baltimore Orioles. Now we weren't just hanging with the best teams in the league, we were ahead of them. We played the Orioles tightly that year. In fact, one of the reasons we were able to get a lead on the Orioles that year was the fact that we had just taken two out of three games against them. The Orioles had been, and were, the class of the American League East and we were hanging with them and beating them. In those disappointing years from 1971 through 1973, we hadn't been as competitive against the Orioles. Now we were.

One of the best catches I ever made came at Shea Stadium and it came against the Orioles. I always enjoyed playing against the best competition. I remember Bobby Grich hitting a long fly ball to left that I went over the wall to catch and rob him of a home run. Over the years, I became somewhat known for plays like that—jumping high over the outfield wall to make a catch and rob a player of a sure four-bagger.

The guy I really wanted to get, though, was the gifted centerfielder on the Orioles, Paul Blair. I had known Paul from our days as kids in Los Angeles. As a Major Leaguer, Paul had become one of, if not the best, centerfielder in the league. He covered a lot of ground, and he made tremendous catches all the time. He won eight Gold Gloves, and at one point (from 1969-75), he won that award seven consecutive years.

Back in the early 1970s, I was enjoying one of the best hot streaks of my career. I had driven in runs in a number of games in a row, maybe seven or eight. I came up late in a game against the Orioles and hit what was, or should have been, a three-run homer to give the Yankees the lead. I remember watching Merv Rettenmund, the right fielder, going back and seeing the ball soar over his head as I got to first and rounded the bag. And then, seemingly out of nowhere, Paul Blair appeared deep in the outfield. He went back to the wall and leaped high to catch the ball that was well over the fence and robbed me of a home run. As he ran off the field, I saw him and told him that I would get him back. I never did. And Paul never stopped reminding me of that catch. One year at a fan fantasy camp, many years after we retired, he actually showed up with a photo of that catch. He showed it to me, and said, "Remember this, Roy?" I was always glad to rob Orioles players of home runs, and I figure I got many of them over the years, but I never did get back at Paul Blair!!

As the 1974 season was winding down, the Orioles came into Yankee Stadium for a big three game series. We were in first place by two games. We were getting hyped up that we'd win the division and be in the playoffs. It was here though that the Orioles flexed their muscles, sweeping us in the series, winning games by the scores of 4-0, 10-4, and 7-0. After that series, we found ourselves in second place one game out. As they had been doing to us for years, the Orioles demonstrated that they were still the better team.

Still, we didn't give up and proved to be resilient and we re-captured first place again, briefly, after sweeping the Indians. It was like that as the season wound down. It was a tight race. Every single game had meaning. With just two games to play, we found ourselves in second place, but we were only one game out. We were confident heading into the last two games because we had won four games in a row. We were to play those last two games against the Brewers in Milwaukee. The Brewers were in second to last place. They were just playing out the string. If ever we were ready to win a few more games, this seemed to be the time.

As we were leaving Cleveland after sweeping the Indians, our flight was delayed for a few hours and some players passed the time at the bar. The drinking probably continued on the flight. Then, by the time we arrived at the hotel, two of our reserve players, both catchers, Rick Dempsey and Bill Sudakis, ended up in a situation where words must have been said and taken very seriously. A fight erupted between these two right in the lobby of the Pfister Towers Hotel in Milwaukee. This was a serious ruckus that a number of players rushed in to break-up, including Bobby Murcer. Neither Dempsey nor Sudakis were injured, but Bobby was. He hurt his thumb and couldn't play. Bobby's season was over.

The following day, we lost the game, the next-to-last game of the season, 3-2 in ten innings. I'll always wonder how things might have been different if Bobby had played and we won that game. We did win the season's last game, but we ended up finishing in second place. Close, but no cigar. It was a disappointing way for it to all end.

More than in 1970, when we had last come this close to winning the American League East, this finish felt like a true signal that we were on our way. There was no champagne shower in the locker room. Finishing second in 1974 didn't feel good. We were a good enough club to win the division. We had set high expectations and we were living up to that high standard.

In 1974, Bill Virdon batted me lead off. We had a number of excellent players who started coming into their own behind me in the batting order—guys who would become the heart of the championship teams. Graig Nettles hit 22 home runs and drove home 75 runs. Lou Piniella hit .305 and drove home 70 runs of his own. Thurman Munson played a steady catcher. I had a steady year batting .275. I walked 67 times and my On Base Percentage of .367 put me in the top-ten players in the league. I even appeared on the cover of *The Sporting News* again this time with the caption "Leadoff Artist."

It's interesting that we remember one player as having a down year in 1974. It was a career changing year. That player was Bobby Murcer. In 1974, he hit only 10 home runs. Ever since becoming a starter, Bobby hit 20 or more home runs year after year. One year he topped 30. Bobby had a perfect swing for the short right field porch at Yankee Stadium, and he hated playing at Shea Stadium where the walls were deeper and many would-be home runs became nothing more than long outs. All season long, Shea Stadium got into Murcer's head. He hit only two home runs there, and they both came (on back-to-back days) in the season's final days. Still, Bobby drove home 88 runs to lead the team. People don't remember that Bobby actually did that well. Bobby even hit over .300 in our home games, but everyone seems to only remember the fact that he hit so few homers, especially at home.

1974 was also a transition year for Bobby because he was moved from centerfield, where he had played for years, and was often referred to as the "next Mickey Mantle" to right field since we had acquired a gifted defensive centerfielder in Elliott Maddox. There were few players in baseball that could cover the ground that Maddox could. He was that good.

And then, of course, came that fight in Milwaukee that ended Bobby's season early. All in all, it wasn't a good year for him. And then it got worse.

That winter, the Yankees made a blockbuster trade with the San Francisco Giants. My teammate and friend, Bobby Murcer, a Yankee star, was sent to the Giants in exchange for one of baseball's most gifted players, a big star of his own, and as much a part of the Giants as Bobby was a part of the Yankees, the great Bobby Bonds. We didn't want Bobby Murcer to go but knowing that Bobby Bonds was to be a Yankee provided us with anticipation for what the 1975 season might bring. Looking back though, I have to wonder how much greater of a star Bobby Murcer would have been if he had never left the Yankees and if the Yankees had never left Yankee Stadium. In a different ballpark, if he had been home, we might have won the pennant in 1974.

That winter, the Yankees also signed the first big free agent player, future Hall of Fame pitcher Jim "Catfish" Hunter. Having Catfish as the ace of our staff also brought with it great anticipation.

Things were changing. We knew 1975 would be our last in Shea. We'd now also had two bona fide superstars, Bonds and Hunter, on the team. That winter, I resumed my karate training with great anticipation for what was to come.

***

Bill Virdon had a surprise for me as Spring Training began in 1975. He called me into his office and said that I was going to have to play first base—that I would be in a platoon with our regular first baseman Chris Chambliss who had arrived in 1974 in a huge trade with the Indians that sent a number of long time Yankees, including Fritz Peterson, to Cleveland. Chris, the American League Rookie of the Year in 1971, was a good player, but he struggled for the Yankees in 1974, batting under .250 and not hitting home runs as the Yankees thought he should. Virdon figured that I could provide the right-handed hitting to complement Chambliss' left-handed swing. I wasn't thrilled about this move. I had figured that, by now, I was established as an outfielder. Chambliss also wasn't thrilled, I'm sure, as he saw himself as an everyday player and not someone who should be platooned. Chris, though, was a true professional and a great teammate. So that I could try my hand at playing first, he even loaned me his glove.

In the fifth or sixth Spring Training game, a few weeks into camp, I was playing first base against the Twins in Orlando. I tried to make a diving play on a ball to my right and dove awkwardly. I landed on my glove hand side. It was originally thought that I sprained my thumb, so I came out of the game. The next day I went for an ultrasound and an x-ray. It was more than a sprain. I had a hairline fracture in my thumb. My hand was bandaged up and for the remainder of Spring Training and I couldn't catch balls or swing a bat. All I could do was work to get my legs in shape.

Over the course of a season, things have a way of working out. Once the season started and I was able to hit, I put a sponge on my bat to lessen the pain from swinging and hitting the ball. There are a lot of aspects of the game that fans don't necessarily know, or they forget from their own playing days as kids. When a baseball bat connects with a ball, there is a reaction that the batter feels on his hands and sometimes up his arms. On cold days, it often hurts one's hands when he makes contact. When facing a pitcher throwing 90 miles-per-hour, that contact can really sting. In my career, most players didn't wear batting gloves. I never did. I appreciated the feel of the wood bat in my hands. One aspect of Spring Training is getting your hands callused and ready for the long season. Interestingly, because of the dynamics of a swing and the way a player's hands go through the hitting zone, ironically, I also knew that if I swung and didn't make contact, my thumb was going to hurt even worse. This made me bear down and focus just a little more.

I appeared in the game on Opening Day as a pinch runner but didn't play in any games for another week or so as my thumb still needed time to heal. Once I was playing, the Yankees had me leading off playing left field one day and at first base the next. I got off to a hot start and things were going well. Lou Piniella and Chris Chambliss were also sharing first base duties with me, but Piniella came down with an ear infection, possibly vertigo, and started missing time. Chambliss then started playing more and more and he finally proved to Bill Virdon that he could hit lefties. That sent me back to left field permanently. All in all, I played only seven games at first base in 1975, and I never played there again.

We had high expectations for that 1975 season, but our team never seemed to get going. We played below .500 ball in April and May. Bobby Bonds was struggling as the cleanup hitter. Even though I was doing well as a leadoff batter, Bill Virdon moved Bonds there as a way to hopefully get him going. I was moved to the third spot in the order. A lot seemed to be in flux, and a lot wasn't working.

I loved playing with Bobby Bonds. He was a special ballplayer with tons of talent—the typical "five-tool" player. He could hit for average. He had tremendous power. He could run. He was also a great fielder with a strong throwing arm. Talent like Bobby Bonds' just doesn't come around often. But there's more to a team than just putting the most talented players together on a baseball field. Team chemistry is important. When players play together for years and years, they get to know each other, things sometimes feel more natural. There's a flow. Bobby Bonds was a great teammate, but I think the team missed Bobby Murcer and his professionalism and leadership. It didn't feel right to have our version of Mickey Mantle playing in San Francisco.

Catfish Hunter also didn't get off to a good start. He lost his first three games, and the Yankees lost the first four games he started that year. Amazingly, the great Jim Hunter was being booed by the fans. I understand how the fans want players to perform, but it's not always easy to come to New York and perform under the bright lights of the city. I don't think the negative reaction from the fans helped Catfish pitch any better. He was able to turn it around, but not every player can do this. It takes a very special kind of player to excel in New York.

We were not living up to the expectations, our own or the fans'. Meanwhile, the Boston Red Sox had two dynamic rookies who were tearing the league apart. Fred Lynn and Jim Rice were having tremendous years helping the Red Sox win their fair share of games. The Milwaukee Brewers also got off to a hot start. By the middle of May, the Yankees were in last place. It was shaping up as a long season. This was reminding me of the big step backwards we took as a team after that successful 1970 season. I wondered if we were doomed to more years of mediocrity. But with the talent around me, I just didn't think this was possible.

I was always known as a calm player, but by early June, in a series against the White Sox in Chicago, I lost my cool. I had been hitting the ball hard, but right at guys and I was in a frustrating slump. I came up late in the game with a runner on third and one out and was looking to drive him home. Now, they don't call Chicago the windy city for nothing. I hit a good fly ball to deep enough right field to score the run, but the wind pushed the ball back toward the infield and it ended up as just an out and the runner could not score. I was so mad that I took out my frustrations on the water cooler. First, I hit it with my forearms and then I kicked and punched that thing and knocked it off the wall. That's when the water pipes burst. Water was flying everywhere. This made me even angrier. I grabbed that thing and threw it down the stairs. The other players scattered. When I went out to my position after that I was soaking wet. Later the White Sox General Manager, Roland Hemond sent me a note that said my work on that water cooler was impressive. It might have been, but he also sent a fine. I don't remember having to pay the fine. What I do remember is that the next time we were in Chicago, the water cooler was bolted to the wall. After that a number of my teammates said, "If we ever get into a fight, we want to stand next to you."

We did turn it around for a short time in June, winning twenty games, but after winning just eleven games in July, Bill Virdon was fired as the manager. He was fired for two reasons. First, obviously, we were not performing. Secondly, the Texas Rangers had fired their manager a short time before. That manager, Billy Martin, was just who George Steinbrenner felt the Yankees needed. And, in many ways he was. Billy Martin was a fiery manager. He got the most out of his players. And he was a Yankees legend of sorts. Billy was the second baseman on many Yankees teams in the 1950s. He wasn't a star, but he knew how to win. He brought that approach as a player to his managing. Billy was a big personality. George loved big personalities. It was Billy who would bring us to the World Series in 1976 and 1977, but, of course, not without a lot of turmoil and back page newspaper headlines along the way.

We all know of Billy Martin and his reputation as an emotional guy. He was also a brilliant manager. When Billy came, the first thing I noticed was the way he managed. His approach was different from everyone else. He didn't do things by the book. He was always doing things to outsmart the other teams. Billy was a genius when it came to baseball smarts, strategy, and knowledge. He was always a few steps ahead of the other team. Other managers tried to out-think Martin, but they couldn't. Billy Martin's smarts gave us a huge edge.

I remember learning of Billy's unconventional ways in one of our first games with him as the manager. We had runners on first and second. I was the guy on second. They gave the bunt sign to Piniella on the first pitch, but he didn't get it down. On the next pitch, I assumed the bunt was still on and waited for him to make contact before running. Piniella, instead of bunting, swung, got a hit, and I scored. I came into the dugout and got the congratulations from my teammates—handshakes, back slaps, high fives, and all of that. Then Billy came over and asked, "Do you know you just missed a hit and run?" No one had ever called a hit and run in that situation before. No one except Billy Martin. That's when I knew things were going to be different. I scored a big run and Billy Martin wasn't happy with me. I made sure to not miss any signs after that!

Overall, we went 30-26 under Billy Martin and ended the 1975 season in third place. Our 16-10 finish in September left us confident that the next year would be even better!

One of my early at bats in Little League.

My mom and I in the early 1970s.

My father at an art studio.

Mickey Mantle and me by the batting cage, 1968.

It was always great when kids asked me for my autograph.

I became known for uniform #6, but early in my career, I wore number 48.

Photo courtesy of the National Baseball Hall of Fame and Museum.

Elston Howard, Willie Mays, and me at the All-Star Game.

Family Day at Yankee Stadium with my wife Linda and daughter Loreena.

Family Day at
Yankee Stadium
with my son Reade.

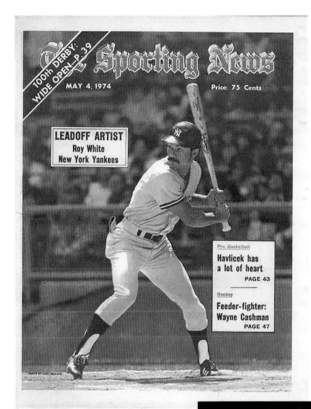

On the cover of *The Sporting News*, May 4, 1974. Image courtesy of *The Sporting News*

Being a "Leadoff Artist" meant I got on base a lot. I always loved base running and stealing bases.

Photo courtesy of the National Baseball Hall of Fame and Museum.

Bobby Murcer, Curt Blefary, and me taking instruction from manager Ralph Houk.

This flyball got away from me.

After the 1973 season karate became a part of my off-season training.

I even made the cover of *Official Karate* magazine in 1975.

Image courtesy of *Official Karate* magazine.

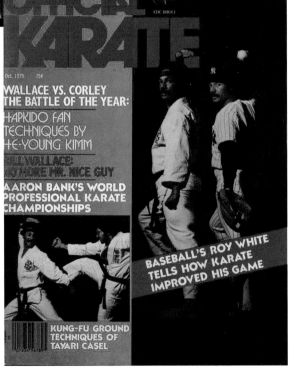

CHARLTON PUBLICATION

Oct. 1975   75¢

WALLACE VS. CORLEY
THE BATTLE OF THE YEAR:

HAPKIDO FAN
TECHNIQUES BY
HE-YOUNG KIMM

BILL WALLACE:
NO MORE MR. NICE GUY

AARON BANK'S WORLD
PROFESSIONAL KARATE
CHAMPIONSHIPS

BASEBALL'S ROY WHITE
TELLS HOW KARATE
IMPROVED HIS GAME

KUNG-FU GROUND
TECHNIQUES OF
TAYARI CASEL

Roy White Baseball Cards Through the Years

1966

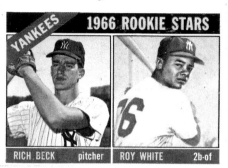

1968

1969

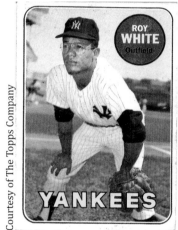

1970

1971

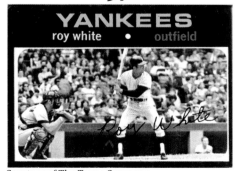

1972

1973

1974

1975

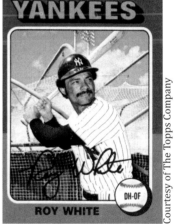

1976

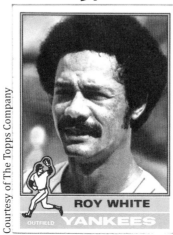

1977

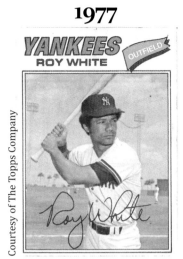

1978

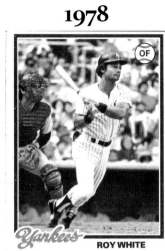

1979

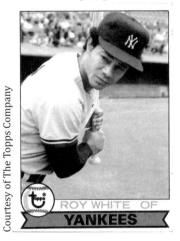

1980

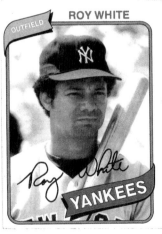

Thurman Munson and me at Spring Training finishing a workout.

There aren't many photos of me as a first baseman. Spring Training 1974

My first acting venture as Dr. Larabee in *The Premonition*.

Me with Rawley Eastwick and Steve Garvey at The Superstars competition.

I caught this one!

Billy Martin congratulates me after a game winning home run.

Batting in the 1978 World Series.

I hope this was a base hit.

The Japanese media greeted me as soon as I got off the plane in Tokyo.

It was a great experience playing for the Yomiuri Giants, the greatest team in Japan.

Having a conversation with a baseball legend (Joe DiMaggio) in Japan as part of the World Children's Baseball Fair.

Paul Semendinger and me at a recent Roy White Foundation event.

Playing on the Yankees with Roy White
By Chris Chambliss

Chris Chambliss and Roy White were teammates on the Yankees for six seasons, from 1974 through 1979. Chambliss came to the Yankees in a big trade the team made with the Cleveland Indians. The Yankees sent pitchers Fritz Peterson, Fred Beene, Tom Buskey, and Steve Kline to the Indians for Chris Chambliss, a first baseman, and pitchers Dick Tidrow and Cecil Upshaw. Chris Chambliss and Dick Tidrow would be important contributors to the Yankees' American League pennant in 1976 and their World Championships in 1977 and 1978. In 1976, Chris Chambliss hit one of the greatest home runs in Yankees history when his blast in the bottom of the ninth inning propelled the Yankees to the World Series.

***

ROY WHITE WAS A great teammate. The best description of him that I can give is that he was a steady influence. Roy White was a dependable person all the way around, both as a player and a friend. While he was never a vocal cheerleader, everything he did was solid. It all made a lot of sense. Because he was so professional and so steady, he was a person others looked to as a leader. I know I did.

I came to the Yankees at the start of the 1974 season. In order to acquire me, the Yankees traded a bunch of pitchers, a lot of guys who had many friends on the team. I had just gotten married too. It wasn't an easy time to be traded. It was a time of great change for me and the Yankees. It eventually all worked out but at the time, it was hard. And, at the start, I didn't perform as the Yankees had hoped. My average wasn't great, and I didn't hit a lot of home runs. I was fortunate that there were players like Roy White around who were professionals.

Roy was a star on the Yankees back then. He was the left fielder for so many years—a solid guy and a solid player. When I met Roy, we hit it off right away. We were both quiet guys who just did our jobs.

I remember that before my second season in New York, Bill Virdon, the manager, had decided to try Roy White and Lou Piniella at first base to platoon me because he didn't think I could hit left-handed pitching. When I first came over, he had told me that I was the guy at first base, but he started platooning me with guys like Bill Sudakis and Otto Velez pretty quickly. It was no surprise that they were looking to find other first basemen in 1975. I was certain that they were looking to trade me away that spring, and they might have, but Roy got hurt after diving for a ball and Lou Piniella came down with an ear infection and vertigo. They had to play me. And that year I started well and just kept hitting. I batted over .300 that year.

Late in 1975, Billy Martin took over as the manager and he played me all the time. My playing time at first base was solidified. It was under Billy Martin that I started driving in 90 runs a year.

When Roy White tried his hand at first base, I loaned him my glove. I didn't hold it against Roy that the manager was trying him there. I probably lent a glove to Piniella as well. This is just what we did. It's about the team. You do what you have to do. I did the same thing for Thurman Munson when he tried out first base late in his career.

If Roy White had played first base, I would have been happy for him because he was a good guy, a friend, and an important player on the team. He was a player who could do so much. He put the ball in play. He could run. He hit for power on occasion. Roy did it all. We needed players like Roy White if we were going to be successful. He was a leader. There was never any "stuff" with Roy. When he talked, it was always the truth. It always made sense. And it always was designed to help us and make us better.

A lot of people remember those late 1970s Yankees teams for the players with the big personalities like Reggie Jackson and Thurman Munson. They also think of Billy Martin and George Steinbrenner. But it was the quiet guys like Roy, and Willie Randolph too, the players who were calm and professional that gave us the needed balance to be successful. As a team, we played rough on the field, and were rough together in the clubhouse. Teams need a little of everything—humor, intensity, big personalities... Over the course of a season, you appreciate the fun element, but without professionals like Roy White, I'm not sure that we would have been successful.

Roy was a leader in so many ways. I have talked about his calming influence on the team and his professionalism, but over a long season, or a career, sometimes emotions do get the better of us. Roy almost never got mad, but there was a game I remember in Chicago at Comiskey Park where Roy lost his temper. Things hadn't been going well for him and he took it out on a water cooler. He really messed that thing up. Roy was into karate then and we saw him do things to that water cooler—chops and kicks and such. It was out of character, but understandable. Baseball is a tough game. We've all felt like that at some point. I still talk to Roy about that sometimes.

Roy White was a great Yankee. He's a special friend. When I see him, it's like we hadn't been apart, we pick right back off where we left off. He was a true champion.

The Yankees as an organization don't seem to understand how important Roy White was to the team. He has not received the recognition he deserves. He's a career Yankee. An elder statesman. A very special guy. He deserves some recognition from the Yankees. It's time.

Chapter 8
The First World Series
1976

EADING INTO THE 1976 season, we were very confident. For one thing, we knew that we would have Billy Martin as our manager for the full year. We knew that alone might make all the difference. Billy was a winner. The teams he had managed were always very competitive. Billy's style of ball also made the players play better. He was always expecting more of the players. And, at least in the short term, the players always responded. Billy had a reputation for creating controversy, as well, but in 1975, we didn't see any of that.

Our main opponent, the Boston Red Sox, were a powerhouse. They were the league champs in 1975 who just lost in one of the most amazing World Series ever. We knew they were eager to get back and win it all. The Red Sox were loaded with a ton of great players, but we felt we could be as good, or better, than them. 1976, we felt, could be our year. It was time. Our time. Finally.

While we had a solid roster, our team was also situated to be even better in 1976. Bobby Bonds was a great player, but he was a bit of a disappointment with the Yankees. After the 1975 season, the Yankees traded him to the California Angels for two players who would be important parts of our championship core—centerfielder Mickey Rivers and Ed Figueroa, a starting pitcher. The Yankees also made a trade with the Pittsburgh Pirates that brought us the great young second baseman Willie Randolph along with Dock Ellis, another quality starting pitcher.

I was excited that I would have Mickey Rivers batting in front of me. He was very fast, one of the quickest players in the league. He stole bases. I knew Rivers would create lots of action and that I'd be able to hit the ball through the holes in the infield that he created. This was my kind of baseball.

What also pleased me was that Billy Martin told me that I had the "green light" to steal whenever I wanted to. If I was on base, I could go at will. I had never been given that kind of freedom on the base paths before. Previously, I always had to wait for the steal sign to be given, and the Yankees, well, traditionally, they just didn't steal many bases. The Yankees were the Bronx Bombers, after all. It wasn't like Babe Ruth, Lou Gehrig, Joe DiMaggio, and Mickey Mantle earned their fame by running.

This was to be a new Yankees approach. A new style. I was very excited for the season to begin.

Physically, I felt I was still in some of the greatest shape of my life, although after 1975, I had given up karate. I knew it wasn't smart to take the chance of getting injured in a sparring session. As much as I enjoyed the physical and mental aspects of karate, I knew I had to give it up. Teams were also becoming less and less tolerant of players being involved in dangerous physical activities in the off-season. Back in 1967, Jim Lonborg, who had just won the American League Cy Young Award for the Boston Red Sox, injured himself skiing. He was never the same player after that. I didn't want to jeopardize my playing career with an off-season hobby—no matter how much I enjoyed it.

As players, many of us took part in all sorts of physical activities in the off-season. We were athletes, after all. For many years, I played in a lot of charity basketball games with a host of big league players including Johnny Briggs, Gene Michael, Ed Kranepool, and Jeff Torborg. We'd play events for local schools and other organizations and walk away at the end of the night with a hundred bucks for our efforts. This was a way to stay in shape and make a few off-season dollars along the way. Gene Michael was an exceptional basketball player.

As player contracts increased, the teams started putting it

in the contracts that if you got hurt doing non-baseball activities, you wouldn't get paid. They even named a few sports that we couldn't play. That list involved playing basketball... and skiing. I don't recall that karate was on the list. Not too many players did karate, but I wasn't going to take any chances.

Billy Martin ran a good camp in Spring Training. He treated us like the pros we were. He knew that we knew how to get ready for the season and we knew that we had to get into baseball shape. And we did. I sure didn't miss those killer workouts that Bill Virdon put us through.

As I looked around at that team in Spring Training, I knew that we'd be good. We all did. There was plenty of talent. Mickey Rivers added the speed element. Willie Randolph was an up-and-coming star. We saw that clearly. And, of course, there were players like Graig Nettles, Chris Chambliss, who had come into his own, Lou Piniella, and Thurman Munson— all no-nonsense hard-nosed players who were ready to win.

On the pitching side, we had Catfish Hunter who was our ace starting pitcher along with the great Sparky Lyle leading our bullpen. I was glad we now had Dock Ellis and Ed Figueroa in our starting rotation. Figueroa was a guy I just couldn't hit. And now he was on our side. I was always glad when that happened. When these guys were my teammates, I wouldn't have to try to hit them.

Billy Martin was a manager who tried to control everything. He was always thinking, always trying to outsmart his opponent. He was good at it. But, as much control as he had, he didn't know everything that we did as players. It wasn't long before Mickey Rivers and I, unbeknownst to Billy Martin, created our own sign. If I touched my batting helmet while he was on first base, that was our own sign for him to steal second. I gave him that sign knowing that it would open a bigger hole for me to hit the ball through. This worked often. Our goal, between Mickey and I, was to get Thurman Munson, who batted third that year, an easy run batted in by having a man on third for him with less than two outs. We wanted to do this as often as possible, especially in the first inning. It worked, too. That year, Mickey scored 95 runs. I had 104 runs scored of my own, which ended up leading the American League, so between just the two of us, we scored 199 times. This also worked out well for Thurman. He batted .302 and drove in 105 runs, the most he ever had in a season. That year, Thurman Munson would win the Most Valuable Player Award for the American League.

I remember 1976 as being a particularly fun season. We lost on Opening Day, but we then won five straight. After the third game of the season, we were in first place—a position we never relinquished. We just put it all together and really started to play the kind of baseball we knew we were capable of playing.

By the end of May, we had a five-game lead in the standings. By late June, our lead was up to nine games. This was our season, and we knew it. I only remember one bad stretch; it came in late July into August. We lost eleven of fifteen games over a couple of weeks. We had a big cushion as we started losing, but as we lost, our division lead kept dwindling. What had once been a 14.5 game lead had quickly dropped to 8.5 games. Things like that can get out of control very quickly.

The game that turned it all around again took place on August 10 in Kansas City against the Royals, a powerhouse team also leading their division by a wide margin. This team was destined to become one of our biggest rivals over the next many seasons and throughout the remainder of my days as a Major League player.

In that game, we were tied with the Royals with only one run each heading into extra innings. You just don't see games like this any longer. Dock Ellis pitched 10 innings for the Yankees. Andy Hassler did the same for the Royals. But then, in the top of the eleventh inning, Thurman Munson homered with two outs to give us a 2-1 lead. Sparky Lyle came in to close it out—and we were back on our way. Including that win, we won eight of our nine games to create a comfortable cushion atop the standings.

We eventually won the American League East by 10 games over the second place Baltimore Orioles, who were also always very good. The Red Sox, who we had been concerned about at the start of the season, ended up in third place, 15.5 games out.

For the first time in my career, I was heading to the postseason. We had come a long way since Fritz Peterson's champagne celebration when we finished in second place in 1970.

We knew that the American League playoffs were going to be particularly tough because we had to play the Kansas City Royals. This was the first of three consecutive years when we would play the Royals in the American League Championship Series. Their team was very similar to ours. It was well-balanced with good power and guys who could run. They had stars such as Amos Otis, Al Cowens, Hal McRae, and the great George Brett. They also had a great staff of starting pitchers that included Dennis Leonard, Larry Gura, a former Yankee, and Paul Splittorff, along with a good bullpen. The Royals, like us, were also very physical. These were two teams, up-and-coming, and full of fight. We knew every game would be tough—a dog fight, nip and tuck, a battle inning-by-inning.

We won Game One behind Catfish Hunter. He pitched one of his best games ever, allowing just four hits and one run over nine innings. He had exceptional control that day. He never went to three balls on any batter. I had a big hit in that game in the ninth inning. Leading just 2-1, I drove home Fred Stanley and Mickey Rivers with a big two-out double to give us a 4-1 cushion.

The Royals then won the second game, we won the third, they won the fourth. It would be like this whenever we'd see the Royals. It just wasn't easy. These were tight games, real battles each game. We didn't give them an inch and they gave none back to us.

The fifth, and final game, the one that would send one of us to the World Series to play the great Cincinnati Reds, would go down as one of the greatest and most exciting games in baseball history.

In that game, The Royals scored first, right away in the first inning. With two outs, George Brett doubled, and John Mayberry followed with a two-run homer off Ed Figueroa. We then came racing back to tie the game in the bottom of the inning. Mickey Rivers tripled. I drove him home with a single. I then stole second and then scored on a sacrifice fly from Chris Chambliss.

The Royals then scored in the second inning, to take a 3-2 lead. This was how we battled. If they scored, we'd score. If we scored, they'd score.

In the third inning, Mickey Rivers singled. I followed with a walk. Thurman Munson then drove home Rivers with the tying run. This was the way Mickey, Thurman, and I had been playing all season. We'd get on base for Thurman to drive us in. I then scored on a Chris Chambliss ground out which gave us a 4-3 lead.

In the bottom of the fourth inning, I thought we might break the game open. Thurman Munson came up with the bases loaded and two outs. Our whole rally that inning actually came with two outs. Fred Stanley walked. Mickey Rivers singled. I then walked again. The Royals went to the bullpen and brought in Marty Patton. Thurman then flew out to left on the first pitch to end the inning.

In the sixth inning, we did it again. Mickey Rivers led off with a bunt single. I then bunted him to second. Thurman drove home Rivers with a hit to right field. This was Billy Martin's type of baseball. This was the style of the 1976 Yankees. Chris Chambliss also scored that inning to give us a commanding 6-3 lead. It seemed that we had the game in hand. There was so much excitement in the stadium. The then-record crowd was going crazy.

But then, in the top of the eighth inning, with two runners on, George Brett hit a loud home run that tied the game at six. It was a deflating moment. We were so close and now, late in the game, it was tied again.

The score stayed that way until the bottom of the ninth inning. Mark Littell was pitching for the Royals. I had faced him the inning before and I hit a rocket, but John Mayberry, at first base and playing the line, caught my line drive easily.

Chris Chambliss led off the bottom of the ninth. He came up and hit one of the most dramatic home runs in Yankees history. It wasn't a no-doubter. We thought it had a chance to go out, but we watched Al Cowens in centerfield and Hal McRae in right going for the ball. As the ball got to the wall, McRae made a leap, and for a long second or two, we didn't know if he had it. Once the ball was gone for a homer, we all went nuts. We ran onto the field, and the fans did as well. Thousands of fans came pouring out of the stands and stormed the field. I got only halfway to home plate before four or five people picked me up. I thought, "I've got to get out of here." It was total chaos. People were streaming all over. I got back to the dugout. Graig Nettles was guarding all the gloves and told us to get them all because the fans were taking whatever they could. It was riotous. Chris Chambliss was mobbed by fans as he was rounding the bases. He was even knocked to the ground. Fans kept grabbing for his helmet. We all rushed to the clubhouse. Chambliss never even had a chance to touch home plate. Later, after 20 or 30 minutes, after they cleared the field of the fans, a police escort came to bring Chambliss out to have him touch home plate. It turned out he couldn't. He could only touch where home plate used to be. The fans, who were taking everything, even took home plate out of the ground!

In the end, this was one of my most thrilling moments in baseball. It was euphoric. After eleven years, we were going to the World Series. When I signed with the Yankees, they were in the World Series almost every single year. And then we hit that long dry spell that I was part of—the only player to play through it all. And, here, finally, we were heading back. When I had first signed with the Yankees, I figured that I would play in many World Series. We had finally made it, and we were going to be playing the Cincinnati Reds, my favorite team from my childhood. Things couldn't have felt much better.

As baseball fans know, the 1976 World Series wasn't much of a contest. After such an amazing finish to the American League Championship Series, the World Series was a letdown for us. The Reds had clinched a few days before, and as such, they were well positioned to be more than ready for the first game. The Yankees, on the other hand, were on a plane heading to Cincinnati the next day after Chambliss' homer. We would only get one day to work out before the first game. When we arrived, the temperature was in the high 30's. It was cold and uncomfortable. It certainly wasn't baseball weather and I think that hurt us.

We also didn't have time to come down and regroup after the dramatic series against the Royals. If we had a couple of days, we could have given a better accounting of ourselves. We also were not set-up pitching wise. Rather than having Catfish Hunter in Game 1, we had to use our number four starter, Doyle Alexander.

Playing in the cold was tough. This was in the days before there were heated dugouts. As I recall, there was a small charcoal pit in the dugout to warm up at. The players would warm their hands there before getting ready to bat. Again, in those days, batting gloves were not in vogue, so it was just your hands and the bat.

On top of it all, the Reds were a great team. They were The Big Red Machine. They had stars aplenty: Joe Morgan, Tony Perez, Johnny Bench, Pete Rose, George Foster, Ken Griffey... on and on. This was a team loaded with talent. Joe Morgan, Tony Perez, and Johnny Bench are all Hall of Famers today. Pete Rose also had a great career. He was a Hall of Fame type player. They were so good in every way. Fans today don't often remember their pitchers, guys like Gary Nolan, Pat Zachary, Jack Billingham, and Don Gullet, but these guys could pitch.

As a team, we just didn't hit. Only one guy was hot— Thurman Munson, who batted .529 in the series, but he couldn't carry us all the way. Mickey and I did nothing, we both hit under .200. The Reds swept us in four straight games.

It was a downer to get swept like that. We were better than that. In the end, even with better weather and a chance to properly prepare, the Reds would have probably beat us, but we could have made it closer. And then, who knows?

And, based upon what happened the next two years, there's at least room to speculate that things might have turned out differently in so many ways.

After the season, many of the Yankees, including me, competed in the Superstars tournament. These pitted sports heroes against each other. There was biking, swimming, bowling, running, tennis, weightlifting, and more. The event ended with an obstacle course. I competed in that competition after the 1975 season as well. In the 1975 competition, I thought I might have a chance in a few of the events. That first year I competed in bowling and tennis on the first day and acquitted myself well. The next morning, before the running race, I woke up with the flu and came in last place.

After the 1976 season, the competition was called the Super Teams competition. The Yankees went up against the Reds again. The competition was in Honolulu, Hawaii and it was great fun. We thought we might be able to get back at the Reds for beating us in the World Series, but they beat us in this competition as well. I remember having some time to talk with Tony Perez and Joe Morgan, guys I played against in the minor leagues. I also remember seeing what a great athlete Ken Griffey was.

Those Cincinnati Reds teams were great, no doubt, they reached the World Series in 1970 and 1972 and had won the World Series in 1975, the season before this one. There was a reason they were called a machine. They were one of the great teams in baseball history. But many people forget that the 1976 World Series was the last one that the Big Red Machine ever reached. I still wonder if we could have ended their dynasty just a few days earlier than it did.

Of course, on the other hand, in 1976, we didn't have Reggie Jackson. He would join the team for the 1977 season. It's possible that he made all the difference.

But it wasn't going to be easy...

The Bronx Zoo years were about to begin.

Chapter 9
World Series Champions
1977

PEOPLE REMEMBER THE **1977** and 1978 Yankees as teams filled with a ton of controversy, chaos, and a lot of winning. These were the Bronx Zoo Yankees, as Sparky Lyle called us. Big personalities filled the clubhouse. Big events occurred on the field. People remember these years as a daily soap opera. That's how much of the story is told and written, but it wasn't all like that. Not always. And not everyone was involved in the daily goings-on. For many of us, we just came to work, played great baseball, and went home.

Not to be forgotten, and most important in the end, these, of course, were the years that the Yankees reclaimed their spot as the World Champions of baseball. There was controversy. There were big headlines in the newspapers. There was tension. But the biggest story of them all was that we won. We were the champions!

The saga of the 1977 Yankees began in late November 1976 with the signing of Reggie Jackson, the game's biggest superstar. Reggie was a winner on the great Oakland A's teams: World Champions in 1972, 1973, and 1974. Besides the Big Red Machine in the National League, the A's were baseball's other great team in the American League. Reggie was the biggest star on that A's team. He was the Most Valuable Player in 1973 and was an All-Star year-after-year.

Thurman and I went to the big press conference at the Sheraton to announce the Yankees' major free agent signing and to welcome Reggie Jackson to the team. From our perspective, we had another great player now on the team—a big home run bat in the middle of the lineup. That was something we had been missing. That was the big thing. With Reggie in the fold, we felt that we'd be in great position to contend and hopefully win the World Series in 1977.

Just like when we acquired Bobby Bonds, one of baseball's biggest superstars would be playing for us. With Bobby, we weren't able to put it together. With Reggie, we did. We knew that all we needed from Reggie, and all we needed from each other as a team, was to play to our abilities. If we did that, we knew we'd win. We just had too much talent. That was a big difference between 1975 (when we had Bonds) and 1977 (when Reggie came aboard). We weren't winners yet in 1975. By 1977, we had tasted the World Series. We knew what it took to get there. And we knew how bad losing in the Fall Classic felt. Reggie also filled a need—we needed a big power hitter.

Reggie was a huge star who also had the biggest of big personalities. What we didn't know or realize at the time of his signing was how much controversy there would be with him. Before becoming a Yankee and coming to New York, Jackson played in smaller markets—Oakland, and for one year, the Baltimore Orioles. In New York, everything with Reggie, the good and the not-so-good, became magnified. Reporters flocked around Reggie Jackson looking for quotes. Reggie was never shy with words. The more Reggie spoke, the more they wrote. It went on and on like this for years.

The first big controversy with Reggie was the comment he supposedly made for *SPORT* magazine where he said that he was the "straw that stirred the drink" and that Thurman Munson could only stir it bad. From my perspective, like so much from this era, this was somewhat overblown. Reggie and Thurman weren't best friends, but they were both winners with the same goal. A lot of what was heard or read then, and even today, was sensationalized. Many of us read the article when it was printed, but I don't recall us all having the magazine in our lockers as it has been portrayed. I was close to Thurman, we had been teammates longer than anyone else on the team, our lockers were right next to each other, and

I don't remember him ever saying anything to me about the article. If it had an impact on Thurman, he didn't talk about it often—or at all. Again, we had a job to do, which was to win baseball games. The other stuff just wasn't all that important to us. It might have sold newspapers. It might have made people tune in to the games or the news coverage on TV. But for us, all we wanted to focus on was winning baseball games.

Reggie was a great player and he helped us win, of course, but he and I never developed a close relationship. Reggie was distant, and not just with me. He seemed to build up barriers between many of the players and himself. That doesn't mean he was a bad guy; it just means he was distant. Reggie Jackson, for good and for bad, was his own person. He made it difficult to befriend him. He didn't joke with us. He usually did his own thing. Our backup catcher, Fran Healy, turned out to be his best friend on the team.

Reggie Jackson added a lot to the 1977 Yankees, but what is often overlooked is the fact that just as the season was about to begin, we also acquired another very important player—Bucky Dent. Bucky was a solid shortstop who had a decent bat. Our shortstops in 1976, Fred Stanley and Jim Mason, were good players, but Bucky Dent was a big upgrade. Bucky was a stronger batter with some pop, and he was a top defensive shortstop. He added a lot to the club. We were really becoming a complete team in every area and in every way.

Before the season, we had also acquired Don Gullet, the excellent pitcher from the Cincinnati Reds. Say what you wish about George Steinbrenner, but he was getting the players that would help us stay competitive. We wanted to win—badly. I think George wanted to win just as much as we did.

When the season began, Reggie started off slowly. After nine games, Reggie was hitting under .200. He eventually came around, of course, but the big hits didn't come immediately. One thing was certain, though, Reggie did the work. If he was in a slump, he'd work out extra hard taking extra batting practice. Reggie would work to drive the ball. He wasn't a home run or nothing guy. Reggie played hard every game. He ran hard on the bases. Reggie was a winner, and it was clear why he was a winning baseball player. This was a dedicated and focused ballplayer. That part of the story never seemed to get told in the papers.

Reggie also knew how to rise to the occasion. I never saw a player have the ability to do this time after time again. If there was a big game on TV, a nationally televised game, Reggie would hit a homer. It became that way. Always. When the eyes were on Reggie Jackson, he responded. The bigger the moment, it seemed, the bigger he became.

Reggie also made us laugh because of some of the things he'd say. He didn't take failure well. I remember a game from 1977, I believe it was against the White Sox early on. We were pounding them. Everyone seemed to have a hit or two. The only guy who didn't get a hit was Reggie. After the game Reggie commented, "Those pitchers only made good pitches against me today." We all got a laugh out of that.

The 1977 Yankees won often enough. We were a good team and were in the race from the start, but we played hot and cold throughout the early months of the season. Billy Martin was inconsistent in his approach. He kept changing the lineup, moving people around. Reggie had a huge ego, but so did Billy, and the two clashed. The Billy Martin of 1977 wasn't the same guy who had managed us to the World Series in 1976.

As Billy toyed with the lineup and changed his approach, I soon found myself moved from the number two spot in the order to batting sixth. That disturbed me because Mickey Rivers (as the leadoff batter) and I had such a great impact the previous season. What we did worked, and we were doing all the things that Billy Martin liked. We played his kind of baseball. I couldn't figure out why he soured on our approach or on me. It was upsetting. My game, as a switch hitter who could put the ball in play from both sides of the plate, hit into gaps, and take walks, as well as being a guy who could run well, was best at the top of the batting order. Why I was moved down in the lineup was never explained to me by Billy who didn't always communicate well.

That was one of the problems and why there seemed to be

so much controversy. Billy Martin just did things. Sometimes Billy would look at a player's long-time history, as he should have with me, and show patience, and sometimes he'd only look at their immediate results. Reggie Jackson, who had been a clean-up hitter for so much of his career, was moved around the lineup. As players, we all felt the uncertainty. It was not the most productive way to play. Players perform best when they are in a comfort zone—when they know what is expected of them. I was mystified. Many of us were. And I wasn't happy with the approach.

Billy's mentor when he played in the 1950s was the great Casey Stengel, one of the most successful managers in Yankees history. In those days, Billy Martin was a second baseman. He was a scrappy player who was known as "Casey's boy." Billy Martin idolized Casey Stengel. In the years he managed the Yankees, they appeared in ten World Series in twelve years, winning seven titles. No team, before or since, has had that much success, not even the Yankees of Babe Ruth and Lou Gehrig. As a manager, Casey Stengel used what he called a platoon system—moving players in and out of the lineup as he worked to get the best match-ups possible. The results were great, no one could argue with the success he had, but as former players told me, Casey was not well liked by many. Many players disliked him because of the lack of respect they felt he showed to them. Looking back at the 1977 season, I think Billy was trying to manage in the way Casey had. The problem was the 1976 approach where we all knew our roles had already been proven to work for us. If Billy Martin had taken that 1976 team and added Reggie to the number four spot in the lineup and left us alone, we might have won even more games. Sometimes you shouldn't mess too much with success.

Many of the players shied away from the almost daily controversy as best as we could, but some events were unavoidable. Some things happened that year that were so out of the ordinary.

There was a game on June 18 in Fenway Park, on national TV no less, where Billy Martin felt that Reggie Jackson didn't hustle for a ball in the outfield. This infuriated Billy. As a result, Martin sent Paul Blair, who the Yankees had acquired the previous winter, out to replace Reggie in the middle of the inning. Things like that just didn't happen. This was a clear case of the manager trying to show-up a player. Reggie came to the dugout, words were exchanged, tempers flew, and Reggie and Billy almost came to blows in the dugout. The coaches and other players had to keep them apart. I watched this situation and the subsequent confrontation in the dugout from the outfield. I had never seen anything like *that* before. This was clearly a case to me of Billy Martin wanting to show up Reggie. By 1977, Jackson wasn't the greatest outfielder any longer, but he was not dogging it on that play. I saw the whole thing from left field. Reggie probably misjudged the flyball, it was off a check swing from Jim Rice, one of the strongest hitters in the game. Reggie played that ball poorly, but it was not for a lack of hustle.

I was usually distant from the negative stuff. I put on the uniform, did my job, and worked to help the team win. I didn't hang around in the clubhouse after the games, so I missed some of the controversy, but, again, much of it was overblown. As people have told the stories, they've grown bigger over the years. That's not to say that it wasn't chaotic at the time, but, for the most part, for most of us, we just came to play ball and stayed clear of the other controversial things that were being written in the papers.

The Red Sox game in Fenway came during a bad slump for our team. We were in the midst of losing seven of nine games. Losing those games caused us to go from being in first place up by two games to being in second or third place. Things were starting to look bad. We were going in the wrong direction and needed to start winning.

On June 24, the Red Sox came into town. The Sox were now five games ahead of us in the standings. With a big series, I am sure they felt they could almost bury us. Even though this was a big series, Billy Martin sat Reggie in the first game. The Red Sox took a 5-3 lead into the bottom of the ninth inning. Reggie got a chance to pinch hit there but this time he didn't come through. He grounded out. But, with two outs, Willie Randolph tripled. I then hit the game-tying home run. We won the game in the bottom of the eleventh inning when Reggie did come through by singling home Graig Nettles.

We won again the next day, and then, in the series finale, we won once again—this time in the bottom of the ninth after I walked, went to third on a Thurman Munson single, and scored on a base hit by Paul Blair. We stopped losing; we turned the tide.

By July 2, we were back in first place. We didn't stay there the rest of the way. These were, after all, tough teams we were battling. We grabbed first place for good on August 23.

I had a solid year in 1977. After the slow start, I also turned it around. I batted over .300 in June and July. For the season, I batted .268 with 14 homers along with 25 doubles. I scored 74 runs, but I'm sure I would have scored a lot more runs had I been batting in my typical number two spot in the batting order. I also might have scored more if I had enjoyed a better September. I finished the season hitting under .200 that month.

The end of the season brought us into another American League Championship Series. And again, it was against the Kansas City Royals.

Just like the previous year, the series with the Royals was hard and intense. It was a true battle. It went back-and-forth. The Royals won the first game. We won Game Two. The Royals won Game Three and needed to win just one more game to eliminate us. But then we won the final two games to take the ALCS and head back to the World Series for the second year in a row.

In the ALCS, the intensity that the two teams showed toward each other came in full display in Game Two. We were ahead 2-1 heading into the top of the sixth inning. With one out, there were runners on first and second. The runner on first was Hal McRae. The next batter, George Brett, hit a bouncer to Graig Nettles at third. Nettles threw to second to get the first out. As Willie Randolph caught the ball, McRae barreled into him, knocking him way off the base and almost into left field. Since Willie was knocked down, Freddy Patek, who had been on second base, raced home to score and tie the game 2-2. We were incensed. Yes, this was hard, old-fashioned baseball, but Hal McRae's rolling tackle into Randolph was too much. Billy Martin and Willie Randolph argued with the umpires that the run shouldn't be allowed to score to no avail. Tough teams though don't just take things like this lying down. In the bottom of that inning, we scored three times to take the lead that would eventually carry us to the victory in that game.

In Game Five, there was another altercation. In the bottom of the first inning, George Brett hit a run scoring triple. As he slid into third base, he came in hard, and Graig Nettles took exception to this. In an instant Nettles and Brett were fighting. The dugouts emptied and we were all involved in a brawl. Baseball brawls are a lot of chaos, people moving fast, pushing, punching, other guys trying to break it up. Unlike today, once the scrum cleared up, both players remained in the game.

The Royals were winning that game 3-1 heading into the eighth inning. In the top of the inning, Reggie singled home Willie Randolph to close the gap to 3-2. But that was only part of the story. Reggie's single came as a pinch-hitter. Billy Martin had benched Reggie in that critical game because Paul Splittorff, a left-handed pitcher, started for the Royals. Even in the biggest of games, Billy Martin was tinkering with the line-up including sitting our biggest star and the single player who most often came through in the biggest moments. Reggie's single brought us closer and once again showed what he could do in the clutch.

We finally took the lead in the ninth inning. I had a small role in that. In the ninth, Paul Blair led off with a single. I then came in as a pinch hitter and drew a walk. Mickey Rivers then singled home Paul Blair to tie the game. Willie Randolph followed with a long fly out—he must have hit the ball 400 feet—to score me from third with the go-ahead run. Rivers scored later that inning to give us a 5-3 lead heading into the bottom of the ninth. Sparky Lyle then closed out the Royals in the ninth innings to win the game and the series for us.

What Sparky Lyle did in that playoff series, and throughout 1977, was amazing. He won the Cy Young Award for his work during the regular season, and I was glad fans across the country could see how good he was in that playoff series. In that final game he got the last four outs of the game, the first to keep us close before our rally and the final three to preserve the win. That was great, but it was what he did the game before, that was truly remarkable. In Game Four, Sparky Lyle pitched more than five innings in relief allowing just two hits along with no walks, and he allowed no runs in a game we had to win and just barely held off the Royals 6-4. This was the way those Yankees teams played.

One negative in that series for me was the fact that, for whatever reason, Billy Martin just didn't play me. Maybe he felt my poor September was a problem. He should have known, though, that players all have good months and bad months. He should have also known that I was ready and able to perform. When I did play (I started one of the games in left field), I came through. I batted .400 for the series. That was the good news. The bad news was that I had only five at bats.

We were now back in the World Series, for the second year in a row. We were much more confident than the previous year. This time we knew we were ready to compete.

The World Series had an added meaning to me. We were playing the Los Angeles Dodgers. We'd be playing our away games in my hometown, in front of my family and friends. This was to be a very special thrill. Billy Martin told me that I would get the starts against the right-handed Dodgers pitchers and that Lou Piniella would start against the left-handers. But in this, Billy wasn't being truthful. I didn't get any starts. I appeared in two games, both losses, as a pinch hitter. That was my World Series experience in 1977. I wouldn't be honest if I said that I wasn't extremely angry about being passed over. That was Billy Martin in a nutshell. He knew how to manage a baseball team. He had just got us to the World Series two years in a row. Unfortunately, Billy didn't always know how to manage people.

That 1977 World Series is remembered for one man—Reggie Jackson. He had a great World Series, but it was in the sixth game that Reggie Jackson put on a display for the ages. He knew how to play on the big stage, that's for sure. In that game Reggie hit three homers off three different pitchers to propel the Yankees to an 8-4 victory and the World Championship. Imagine that. Three home runs in one World Series game, each on the first pitch of the at bat, and each off a different pitcher. Reggie's last home run went into the deepest part of Yankee Stadium's centerfield. It was a moon shot. A tremendous blast. That was Reggie. In the biggest moments he became bigger than life. Only Babe Ruth had done what Reggie did. And to think Reggie did that in the game that won the Yankees the World Series for the first time in fifteen years. Amazing. Also amazing, when Reggie came into the dugout after that last homer, the first person to greet him with the biggest of hugs was Billy Martin.

I was happy that I was now a World Champion. I was happy for my teammates and my friend Lou Piniella who had six hits and three runs batted in to help us in the Series, mostly playing left field. But I was also somewhat bitter. After all those years as a Yankee, and after a successful season, and Billy's promise that I'd play, I watched it all unfold from the bench. Getting benched for the World Series was a slap in the face.

One decision I made that I'm not proud of was the fact that I skipped the World Series victory parade in New York City. I regret not being there to enjoy all of the celebrations and to thank the fans. The Yankees fans have always been great to me. Always. At the time though I didn't really feel part of the team. In a way I felt that they won the World Series, that I wasn't really part of it.

Baseball players live a different life than most people. During the summer, we don't have the opportunity to be with family or travel. Once the 1977 season was over, I took my family, and we went to the Catskills for a nice respite in the mountains. It was great to be far away from the city and to just be a dad and a husband again.

Chapter 10
World Series Champions Again
1978

A S THE 1978 SEASON dawned, I hoped that with a World Championship that maybe some of the pressure would be off Billy Martin, that maybe some of the off-the-field craziness would be over, and maybe some consistent lineups would be established so we could all just focus on playing ball. We were now the best team in baseball. We proved we could do it. Now it was just a matter of playing again to our abilities.

As it turned out, nothing much changed. Controversy still followed the team. Sparky Lyle ended up writing a tell-all book about that season. After winning the Cy Young Award in 1977, the Yankees basically replaced him as our number one bullpen arm with future Hall of Famer Rich Gossage. Graig Nettles commented that Sparky went from "Cy Young to sayonara." While the move might have made some baseball sense, Rich Gossage was a premier pitcher, it also sent a message to us all—if Sparky Lyle wasn't safe, how could any of us be?

In 1977, I was frustrated because my playing time was reduced a bit, and I was dropped down in the batting order. In 1978, Billy Martin stopped playing me for long periods altogether.

I didn't think things for me could get worse, but they did.

I thrived on consistency, yet my season at the start was anything but consistent. I sat Opening Day. Then I played in two games. I then sat a game, played in three games, was benched for two, played a game, and sat for two more. As a switch hitter, this did me no good. A switch hitter needs to play regularly to keep his swing from both sides of the plate sharp. That's also the purpose of being a switch hitter—there's no need to platoon us. We hit against all pitchers. Because of Billy Martin's system, I wasn't getting the consistency I needed, at all. By the end of April, I was hitting .189.

Then, in May, I played in only ten games—for the entire month. I couldn't understand it. In Billy's first year, 1976, I played in 156 games and led the league in plate appearances and runs scored. I was also still the guy who routinely had played in every game the team played—for the entire season. I was a player who played Billy's brand of baseball. But he wasn't giving me a shot.

As a team, we were winning pretty consistently at the start. By the end of May, we were 29-17 which is very good, but the Red Sox were having a dream season, and they were winning more often. In spite of our record, which was one of the best in the Major Leagues, we were three games out. It felt like more. Right from the start, the Red Sox seemed to just be that much better than the field. We knew they were the team we'd have to catch. We also knew they were amazingly good. Those Red Sox teams, with future Hall of Famers Carl Yastrzemski, Jim Rice, Carlton Fisk, and Dennis Eckersley, and other stars like Fred Lynn, were a terrific ball club.

As June started, my place on the bench seemed secured. I hadn't played in a game, in any capacity, since May 18. I finally appeared in a game, on June 3 in Oakland. I had a hit. The next day, I was back on the bench. The team had also started losing. A lot. From the end of May to this point, we had lost five out of six games, and we didn't look good doing it.

After a game in Seattle on this same road trip, I went into Billy's office and complained about my playing time. Billy said he agreed with me and blamed my lack of playing time on George Steinbrenner. Billy then said, "I'm playing you from now on." Now back in the lineup, I went out and hit a home run in a big game that we won 9-1 to avoid being swept by the Mariners. I went out and showed what I was still capable of doing.

The next day, I was back on the bench. That was Billy's

approach. You just couldn't always believe what he said.

It was around this time that I asked to be traded. If I wasn't going to play for the Yankees, I wanted to play somewhere. I wasn't the only Yankee player making this request either.

As a team, we went 14-15 in June. Our inconsistent play had us falling farther and farther back in the standings. By the end of the month, we were nine games out and things were getting tense.

Billy Martin's decision-making wasn't consistent. All of a sudden, in mid-June, I finally started playing regularly and because of that, I was hitting again. From June 11 to the end of the month, I raised my batting average from .207 to .261. I was showing what I could do with regular playing time. If the Yankees played me, I knew I'd help them win.

Around this time the Yankees tried to trade me to the Oakland A's. Maybe Billy Martin started playing me to show-case to other teams that I still had it. But Oakland was one place I didn't want to go. Their dynasty from the early 1970s was over. Most of the stars were long gone. Reggie Jackson and Catfish Hunter were Yankees. Joe Rudi was on the California Angels. Vida Blue was on the Giants. Gene Tenace and Rollie Fingers were on the Padres. Bert Campaneris was on the Texas Rangers. On and on.

The 1978 Oakland A's were not a good team. In 1978, they would finish 69-93. In 1977, they finished in last place, behind the Seattle Mariners who were a first year expansion club. The glory days in Oakland were over and I didn't want to be any part of what they had become. On a personal note, I couldn't mention this to my son Reade who was a big A's fan at the time. He might have wanted me to go!

Oakland was also an awful place to play. The stadium sat empty. And it was cold in Oakland for the night games. The players there just weren't happy. Jerry Kapstein was my agent and he called me to tell me that a big deal was made between the Yankees and the A's. I thought about it all, but as a 10 and 5 guy, I refused. Players who were in the league for ten years and for their last five with the same club could refuse a trade. I exercised that right. I wasn't happy with the Yankees at that point, but I certainly wasn't going to let them ship me to baseball's Siberia. After I exercised my 10 and 5 rights, Jerry Kapstein called me and said that the owner of the A's, Charlie Finley, wanted to talk to me. I refused. There was nothing he could say that would make me change my mind. After all, he was the guy who sold all his stars to the other teams.

And then our crazy season got even crazier...

Even after the 1977 World Series and all of Reggie's heroics, he and Billy Martin never really patched things up. There always seemed to be something going on between Reggie and Billy. In July there was a situation that revolved around Billy Martin telling Reggie to bunt in a tie game against the Royals in extra innings. Reggie, a big power hitter, was offended. He followed the sign and tried to bunt and was unsuccessful. Billy then took off the bunt sign, but Reggie kept trying to bunt and popped out to the catcher. The Yankees lost the game in the eleventh inning. For disregarding his manager, Reggie was suspended for five games.

While Reggie was out, Thurman Munson was moved to right field. I had been back on the bench, but now I was given part time designated hitter duties. This is what it had become. We had an outfielder playing DH while we had our catcher playing in the outfield. I hit well in the games I played, as did everyone it seemed, and the team won every game while Reggie was out. That didn't mean that the moves actually made much sense.

Then, while we waited at the airport in Chicago following another win, and on our way to play the Royals, Billy had a few too many drinks and made some disparaging remarks about both Reggie Jackson and George Steinbrenner. The next day, in tears, Billy resigned as the manager of the Yankees.

This wasn't like anything I had lived through before. I stayed out of most of the controversies, and as I have shared, I think a lot of it was overblown and exaggerated, but then again, I had never before seen the manager fighting with his players, constant lineup changes, and the media looking everywhere to write about the latest controversies. Most of us ignored a lot of the chaos, or we became immune to it, but this we couldn't ignore. Billy Martin was now out, and we'd be getting a new manager.

Our new manager had himself recently been fired by the White Sox. He was an old school type of manager, the type of leader who trusts the players, puts out a consistent lineup, and just lets the guys play. This manager was Bob Lemon, who had been a Hall of Fame pitcher from the Cleveland Indians in the 1950s. Lem was laid back. He respected the ballplayers. With Bob Lemon at the helm, a certain professionalism returned to the team. Overnight, the team was completely different. Everything had changed.

And, all of a sudden I was playing regularly again. It's no surprise, but with steady play, I got my swing back. Under Bob Lemon, I hit .286 the rest of the way, but it wasn't just me who was able to turn things around.

When Bob Lemon took over in late July, we were still about 10 games behind the Red Sox. But with a calmer atmosphere, we could go about our business playing baseball. Lemon was the right guy at the time to come in. He didn't do anything drastic. He didn't overreact. He just let us play. We all appreciated the fact that Bob Lemon was a straight shooter. He brought the calm we needed to just focus on baseball.

And the wins started to come...

We went 6-3 for the rest of July. At the end of the month, we were 7.5 games back. And, just as we started playing well, the Red Sox seemed to start losing.

Thurman Munson and I would talk at our lockers every day. "If we keep playing like this, we can catch those guys," Thurman would say. We started to look forward to a big series with the Red Sox in Fenway Park in early September. If we could get close, we figured we'd catch them in the standings when the head-to-head games came.

We kept winning. We went 19-8 in August and just kept plugging away. To their credit, the Red Sox went 19-10, but this allowed us to slowly get closer.

To start September, heading into the games in Fenway Park against the Red Sox, we won five games against just two losses. The Red Sox won only two games and had lost four. (We had played an extra game due to a doubleheader.) And after our game on September 6, we were right where we wanted or hoped to be. We were four games out heading into the four-game series in Boston. If we could sweep, we'd catch the Red Sox atop the standings. If they swept us, we'd be buried and the 1978 season would be a failure, but that wasn't really on our mind. We came into that series and were ready to go. We knew were going to take it to them.

And we did. We won the first game 15-3. The next day we won 13-2. We won the third game 7-0, and then the series finale 7-4. It wasn't even close. We came in and handed it to them. The Red Sox never had a chance. When the series was over, we were tied for first place.

In that series, we beat the Red Sox by hitting everything. We singled and doubled them to death. In three of the games, the team didn't even hit a home run. We just kept getting singles and doubles all over the place. Almost more impressive than our run totals were the amount of hits we had in each game: 21, 17, 11, and 18. I had eight hits and scored six runs in the four games. We were on fire.

A lesser team than the Red Sox would have folded after that, but they also got hot and it became a nip-and-tuck battle between us until the last day of the season. If we won that last game, we would have clinched the pennant, but we lost 9-2. Catfish Hunter got shelled and didn't even last through the second inning. The Red Sox victory set up one of the greatest games in baseball history—a one-game playoff between the Red Sox and the Yankees, to be played in Fenway Park, to decide which team would win the division and which team would go home. It was all or nothing.

Ron Guidry, who had an amazing season for us, with 24 wins and an ERA under 2.00 was our pitcher. He was going against Mike Torrez, who had won 16 games with the Red Sox. Torrez had been a Yankee the season before. In fact, he was the starting pitcher who pitched a complete game in the final World Series game when we won it all in 1977.

In batting practice, Bucky Dent, who was in a slump—he'd been without a hit in our last four games—said that he didn't feel right. I looked at his bat. He was using the same model bat as one I had given to Mickey Rivers earlier in the season. Mickey liked these bats, but they just didn't feel right for me. Bucky typically used a heavier model bat, but I suggested that he use one of mine as they were a bit lighter. That is how Bucky Dent ended up with a Roy White model bat for the crucial spot late in that game.

Both pitchers were throwing well, but Mike Torrez was a little better, throwing his best stuff and the Red Sox were winning 2-0 heading into the top of the seventh inning. It was getting late, the Red Sox had a good bullpen, and we felt we might be in trouble.

With one out Chris Chambliss hit a single. I followed with a base hit of my own. I always hit my best when I was looking for the breaking ball and would just react to the fastball. Mike Torrez threw me the fastball and I lined it up the middle. The next batter, Jim Spencer, got out, which brought up Bucky Dent.

Bucky had some pop, but he wasn't really a power hitter. He had hit all of four homers that season, and only one since mid-July. Torrez threw a pitch and Bucky hit a high drive to left field. There were two outs, so I was running like hell toward second and also watching Carl Yastrzemski, in left field, tracking the ball. I wanted to make sure I could score if the ball got past him. I was waiting to hear the ball hit off Fenway's Green Monster, but no sound came. I then saw Yaz's head just slump down. I knew the ball was out. We were ahead 3-2! Bucky would forever be remembered for his dramatic home run.

Later that inning, Thurman Munson drove home Mickey Rivers and then in the next inning, Reggie, who always came through in big moments, homered.

Still, the Red Sox kept coming back. We were up 5-2, but the Sox batted back in the eighth inning to make the score 5-4 heading into the ninth inning.

It's always better to be part of the action, in the game, than watching as a player from the sidelines. One thing I didn't understand was that Bob Lemon removed me for defense for that ninth inning. It was nerve wracking watching the Red Sox rally. They had the tying and winning runs on base with two outs and Carl Yastrzemski coming to bat against Rich Gossage. These were two future Hall of Famers battling. All I could do was hold my breath...

Goose threw a fastball that tailed in on Yaz and he popped up the pitch high in the air to Graig Nettles at third. When Nettles finally caught the ball, a long, amazing, crazy, and unlikely season ended with us as the division champs. We ran out onto the field and celebrated, for a brief moment, circling and jumping around Nettles. Unlike the previous seasons, there weren't floods of fans pouring onto the field around us, but we quickly headed to the locker room. As we ran into the dugout, George Steinbrenner had gotten onto the field and was slapping us on the back and congratulating us.

Celebrations in baseball are short-lived. We knew we had to play the Royals again in the American League Championship Series. This was the third year in a row we'd be batting the Royals for the American League pennant.

The games in this series were battles, but we were able to prevail in just four games. My biggest memory is the home run Thurman Munson hit in the third game with us down late 5-4. It was the bottom of the eighth inning, there was one out. I was on first after hitting a single. Thurman then homered deep into the bullpen in Yankee Stadium. Like the Bucky Dent homer, I was running hard to be sure to score if the ball didn't go out, but this blast just kept going. It had to be one of the longest balls Thurman ever hit. That homer gave us the lead 6-5, the score we won by.

The next game, I had my big playoff moment. In the bottom of the sixth inning, I broke a 1-1 tie with a home run of my own to give us a 2-1 lead. That homer turned out to be the winning run in that game and we held off to win by that score. With that win, we were American League Champions again. We were heading back to the World Series for the third consecutive year!

If the 1977 World Series was a disappointment for me, the 1978 World Series was all glory. I finally had a chance to play in front of my hometown in a World Series as we were once again playing the Los Angeles Dodgers. As a team, we stumbled out of the gate losing the first game 11-5 and the second one 4-3 before we turned it around. I was showing that I was able to perform on the big stage by having one hit in the first game and two hits in the second game. I also scored two runs.

The turning point of the World Series came in Game Three when Graig Nettles put on a display of glove work at third base that was among the best ever seen in World Series play. He made great plays to his left and right to rob the Dodgers hitters of countless hits and to save me, in left field, and right behind him, a lot of trouble chasing the hits down. Nettles' glove kept us in the game. I also contributed a first inning home run to give us the lead that we'd never relinquish. Everything started rolling after that. Starting with this game, we won four games in a row to capture our second consecutive World Championship.

I played a lot in that series and demonstrated what I could do. Bob Lemon batted me at the top of the order, usually first or second. In many of the games, it was like it had been in 1976 with Mickey Rivers leading off, me batting second, and Thurman Munson hitting behind us both. It felt good to be in the center of it all, contributing to our winning. I batted .333 for the series with four walks, nine runs scored, and four runs batted in. Those nine runs scored were more than any other player that series. The sportswriters told me that I was in the running for MVP, eventually won by Bucky Dent.

I have only two small regrets. In the final game. Bob Lemon again put Gary Thomasson in left field for the final inning. I would have loved to be on the field when we won it all. Then after the series win, I didn't attend the World Series Victory Parade in New York City.

Sometimes we make decisions in the heat of the moment. In 1977, I didn't enjoy the World Series victory as much because I felt like Billy Martin hadn't been honest with me. I didn't play much in that series and in my frustration, disappointment, and anger I didn't attend the parade. After the victory in 1978, I didn't want to look like a hypocrite, so I again didn't participate in the parade. Looking back now, many years later, I wish I did.

Still, it was a great feeling to be on top. We were the World Champions. I was a major player in our success with some big postseason hits. I had at least one hit in all ten postseason games. I also had at least one hit in eight of the regular season's last nine games. I was the old veteran on the team, the longest-tenured Yankee, but I showed I still had something left in the tank. Bob Lemon put his trust in me, and I responded.

I looked forward, greatly, to the 1979 season.

Playing and Coaching for the Yankees with Roy White
By Willie Randolph

Willie Randolph is considered one of the greatest second basemen in Yankees history. He came to the Yankees in a trade with the Pittsburgh Pirates before the 1976 season. The Yankees then proceeded to appear in the next three World Series. Willie Randolph was a six-time American League All-Star. During his career, he was named co-Captain of the Yankees (along with Ron Guidry). Randolph spent 13 years as a Yankees player. He also played for the Oakland A's, New York Mets, Milwaukee Brewers, and Los Angeles Dodgers. After his playing days, Willie Randolph coached for the Yankees and served as the manager of the New York Mets.

***

I **WAS VERY FORTUNATE** to have the privilege of playing with and coaching with Roy White. We were teammates, colleagues, and friends. We're still friends to this day, and always will be. Roy White is one of the special people in this world. I have been in and around the game for a long time. It's rare that every person has something positive to say about another individual, but it is that way with Roy White. He is universally respected in and out of the game because he is a quality person and was a great teammate and leader.

I came to the Yankees as a player in 1976. I was just a kid, but by that time, Roy White was an established and respected veteran. He was one of the best players on the bad Yankees teams of the late 1960s and had been with the Yankees ever since and was now part of the rising and successful Yankees.

I, of course, knew of Roy White. I had seen him play in person many times at the old Yankee Stadium since I had grown up in Brooklyn and had attended games as a Con Ed Kid. (Consolidated Edison, an energy company in New York, had a program where local kids could attend big league games. The kids who participated were called Con Ed Kids. I was one of them.) We'd sit in left field, so I was able to see Roy White closely. I loved the way he played. He played the game the right way—he was as fundamentally sound as they got.

Years later, playing with Roy White was a dream come true. I initially watched him from afar, but I was honored when he and his friends, guys like Chris Chambliss, took me under their wings. I tried to be cool as a young player, but I was in awe tagging along with Roy White. What an honor! I learned a great deal about the game of baseball, about being a teammate, and about being a good person from Roy.

One of the first things I observed was that Roy got along with everyone. No one said a bad word about him. Those late 1970s Yankees teams were filled with big personalities. There was a lot of laughing and ribbing in the clubhouse and on the team bus, but you just couldn't get on Roy. He was so nice. If in the fun, someone said something to Roy, he'd never come back with a nasty comment. Instead, he'd just laugh. One of those guys everyone loved.

At the time I played with him, the last few years of his career, he and Lou Piniella were platoon-type players. Either could have played full time, but they took their roles seriously. Roy, of course, was instrumental on the World Series teams. He was a leader, a quiet leader, on two World Championship teams. I watched and learned how to be a dignified leader by seeing the way Roy White went about his daily work. I had somewhat of a quicker fuse, but I learned how to stay cool and composed from Roy. I learned how to play the game the right way by watching and listening to him. I learned to chill a bit by being with him. We spent a lot of time talking baseball. I am better because of that.

When Roy White left the Yankees after the 1979 season,

it really hurt me. I felt more alone. He had become one of my dear friends and was someone I leaned on. That was one of my first experiences with a close teammate leaving the Yankees. There was a bit of an adjustment for me and I believe the team as well. In 1979, we, of course, also lost Thurman Munson in that terrible plane crash. As a team, it took us a couple years to get over Thurman. Losing Roy at the end of that year also didn't help.

In short, Roy White taught me how to be a Yankee. I remember trying to figure out who I would go to once he was no longer on the team and playing in Japan.

It wasn't too long that I realized that I had become the established veteran on the team. Because of the example Roy White set, I now wanted to be that same role model and good teammate to the new players. Roy White taught me how to be my best and to lead with quiet dignity—what some might call "class." I feel baseball is all about legacy. And there is a strong and long Yankees legacy. I felt that guys like Thurman, Mel, and Roy were sort of passing the torch on to me. When I was named captain, I was ready to lead. I had been doing that for years, because of what I learned from Roy. If you lead by example, your message comes though. Roy White's leadership came through loud and clear on those great Yankees teams.

Many years later, in 2004 and 2005, Roy and I became teammates of a different sort as coaches on the Yankees. Coaching with Roy White was great for many reasons. Of course, since we were friends and teammates, we already knew and respected each other. We were also part of a terrific coaching staff, under manager Joe Torre, that was comprised of established veterans. Over the years, I learned that not all coaching staffs are cohesive. There can be a lot of insecurity in the game. It wasn't like that with the Yankees when Roy and I were together. On those teams, in part because of Roy's leadership, the coaches all worked well as a unit together. We always shared a lot of things and helped each other. Roy did the outfield. I took care of the infield. But as we did our own things, we assisted each other, and the players.

Watching Roy White coach was a real learning experience. He has a great manner with the players. He communicates extremely well. The players know that he knows what he is talking about. When it comes to teaching hitting, Roy is a guru. The man just knows how to hit and how to help others become better hitters. Coaches can't be effective if the players don't listen to them, but the players always listened to Roy White. He had that quiet presence that commanded, in his way, respect. The players trusted him and worked hard with him.

Roy White is also not a self-promoter. He just went about doing his job. Roy didn't care about who got the credit. He was a winner and he wanted to help the team win. So many players blossomed under his guidance—when he worked in the minor leagues years before and when he coached at the big league level.

Roy White is one of the most special people in the game. Success never got to him. Roy was always the same—a class act. Consistent. True. Loyal. Knowledgeable.

Today, it's time for the Yankees to recognize Roy White and give him an honor he so much deserves. Roy White belongs in Monument Park. Absolutely. When you look at Roy's career, he's up there in the Top 10 Yankees of all-time, on so many lists. You can't tell the story of the Yankees without including Roy White's name. He is that important. Roy White transcended two different eras in Yankees history. I would love to have Roy White join me and the other Yankees who are honored in Monument Park.

Chapter 11
My Last Season in the Major Leagues
1979

SOMETIMES **WHAT WE HOPE** for does not turn out. There was no reason to believe that 1979 would turn out differently for us than the previous three seasons. The Yankees were filled with the same players, all of us young enough to still be at the top of our game. Ron Guidry was the 1978 Cy Young Winner. We had future Hall of Famers Reggie Jackson, Catfish Hunter, and Rich Gossage. Chris Chambliss, Graig Nettles, Willie Randolph, Thurman Munson, Mickey Rivers, Bucky Dent, Lou Piniella and I were all confident that we'd be able to play great baseball. The Yankees also brought in 20-game winner Tommy John and longtime veteran Luis Tiant to make our pitching staff even stronger.

Bob Lemon proved to be just the right manager for this club. The controversies, for the most part, ended. We were the two-time World Champions and were ready to battle all season long for our third straight pennant.

It wasn't to be.

1979 was a disaster on many levels, most of all on a personal level as that was the year we lost our captain, and one of my best friends, Thurman Munson, in a terrible plane crash in August. In all my years in and out of baseball, the day Thurman died was one of the saddest and worst ever. It still hurts to think about it.

Even before that terrible day, 1979 was turning out to be a bad season on so many levels.

In 1979, we never really got it going. After a good enough start that had us tied for first on April 20, things fell apart.

The next day, on April 21, Rich Gossage our ace relief pitcher and Cliff Johnson, a back-up catcher/DH, two big men, got into a scuffle in the shower. The end result was that Gossage tore ligaments in his thumb and was placed on the disabled list. He would be out for two months. Being without Gossage hurt the team. It took away one of our best weapons. Cliff Johnson was soon traded. People have asked me about that fight, but like so much in that time, I only found out about it after the fact. I had so refined my quick exit from Yankee Stadium that I was already on my way home when the scuffle occurred.

By the end of May, we were 4.5 games out. And then in June, we just lost too many games. By June 17, we were eight games out with a 34-31 record. At that point, Bob Lemon was fired. And Billy Martin was brought back. All of this seemed surreal.

Under Billy, my playing time got reduced again. All of a sudden, I was a back-up player used only to pinch hit or pinch run. I could still play left field well, but often when I played, Billy made me the designated hitter. It was all very frustrating.

But the worst day came on August 2, an off day between a series in Chicago against the White Sox and a new series at home in New York against the Orioles. More and more, Thurman wanted to be with family on our days off. He had purchased an airplane to be able to get home quickly each time we had a day off. On this day, while Thurman was home, he took some time to practice take-offs and landings in his new jet. Something went wrong and he crashed and died in a terrible fire. It was devastating.

The news didn't get to the ballplayers at the same time or the same way. There was no Internet or cell phones. The story didn't even get on the television that quickly. There was no cable-TV or 24-hour news. I found out about Munson's plane crash when the writer Phil Pepe called me. For the next long while, much of what happened was a blur. None of this seemed real. I had been teammates with Thurman Munson since 1969. Our lockers were right next to each other. He and I were the only players from the start of this decade to still be with the team. We had gone through it all together. Just the day before we both played in our 9-1 win over the White Sox. And now he was gone? Devastating.

We still had to play the next game, as well, against the Baltimore Orioles on August 3. It didn't seem right. We lost that game 1-0. No one's heart was in it. Not on our team and not on the Orioles. Thurman Munson was a competitor. He played baseball the right way. He was a star who was respected by everyone around baseball. I'm sure the Orioles didn't feel like playing the game that night either.

The Yankees made arrangements for the whole team to fly out to Thurman's funeral which was to be on Monday, August 6. Major League Baseball wouldn't postpone that game either, so we had to fly back home to play that night against the Orioles one last time in that series.

I wanted to play in the game that night. No player had been with Thurman Munson longer than me. Thurman Munson was a guy I sat next to for ten years as a teammate and who was one of my best friends on the team. But Billy Martin had other plans.

One of Thurman's best friends on the team was also Bobby Murcer. Bobby was, of course, traded after the 1974 season. He played for the Giants and then the Cubs, but in 1979, the Yankees brought Bobby back home. That game on August 6, was to be a very special night for Bobby Murcer and the team, and the Munson family as well. Bobby had an amazing night. Earlier in the day, he delivered the eulogy at Thurman's funeral and then he had a huge game against the Orioles driving in all five of our runs as we won in the bottom of the ninth inning. We were all glad for Bobby Murcer being able to pay such a great tribute to our captain and friend in what was the saddest game of my and so many of my teammates' professional careers.

After Thurman died, much of the life was drained from us all. We played our best, but it wasn't the same. There was a huge void that couldn't be filled. We were professionals. We gave it our all, but it's tough to be at the top of your game when your heart has been ripped from your body. To our credit, we had a winning record in August and September. We truly didn't give up, but 1979 was Baltimore's year. We won 89 games, but it just didn't look so good because the Orioles won 102 games and we never really challenged them.

We ended the season in fourth place. It was clear that a lot would now change. For me, the handwriting was on the wall. I knew that I didn't have Billy Martin's confidence. I played in only 81 games that year. That was the fewest I ever had in a complete season since I became a regular in 1968. I had only 205 at bats, the lowest of my career except for that first season, 1965, when I had a small taste of the big leagues. I batted only .215. It was, in so many ways, my worst season ever.

At the end of the season, my contract with the Yankees ended. I was now a free agent. The Yankees made a minimal effort to keep me. General Manager Al Rosen offered me a two-year deal and said that he couldn't offer any more money than he did considering my age. I agreed in principle, but then I learned that the two-year contract the Yankees had offered pitcher Luis Tiant the previous year was for more money each season than what they were offering me. Most players, like myself, didn't focus on what other guys were earning, we were there to play and win. But this upset me. Tiant was older than I was! It turned out that the Yankees were not being truthful with me. They didn't have a maximum salary for players of a certain age, they just told that to me as a negotiating ploy. As a longtime homegrown Yankee, I felt that this was disrespectful. I told my agent, Jerry Kapstein, to try to find me a better deal.

And he did. Jerry Kapstein soon told me that he had a two-year deal for me with the California Angels. This was appealing to me. By signing with the Angels, I'd be able to finish my career close to home, where it all began in Compton. The Angels were also a very good club. They had just been in the playoffs after winning the American League West. (Interestingly the 1979 Yankees with 89 wins actually won more games than the Angels, who won 88, but that's the way it works out sometimes). There was a ton of talent on those Angels teams. The 1979 MVP, Don Baylor, was on the team.

Nolan Ryan was there. And my good friend Rod Carew with whom I always loved to talk baseball was there. This would have been a great move for me.

But the Angels seemed to take me somewhat for granted. They told me that they wouldn't fly me out for a press conference. That turned me off. They didn't even think enough of me to highlight my signing? I soon turned them down and started to wonder where I'd play the 1980 season.

I have been asked if there was a sense that George Steinbrenner didn't go to bat for me, that somehow, he didn't appreciate me as a player. I think initially, George saw me as a player that wasn't quite his style. I wasn't loud as a person or a player. I did my job well, but quietly. I wasn't flashy, like Reggie Jackson, for example. George also loved, at least initially, the players he brought in through free agent signings or trades. These were his players. I predated Steinbrenner. I was a Yankee before he was. I think he needed some time to accept that. In the end though, I believe George Steinbrenner appreciated me for my playing abilities and quiet leadership. I think he knew that the team needed leaders like me too. I was the type of player that some managers and owners only came to appreciate over time. As Bill Virdon once said, "When you see Roy White play every day, you appreciate what he brings to the game." I believe George Steinbrenner felt that way also. I'm sure George would have been happy to have me on the team for the 1980 season. Sometimes things just don't work out.

It was then that long-time major leaguer Lenny Randle called me. I played ball with Lenny growing up. He said that Frank Robinson needed an outfielder for his winter league team in Ponce Puerto Rico. They wanted me to play for them. At the same time, I needed to know if I still had it. I knew I would get some needed at bats and play regularly in the winter league. I happily agreed.

I felt great playing in Puerto Rico, and I did well. And that's where I caught the eye of one of the greatest baseball teams in the world—the Yomiuri Giants of Tokyo. Through my agent I later found out that the manager of the Giants,

Shigeo Nagashima, a Japanese baseball legend, saw me playing in the World Series and stated, "I'd like to have that guy, Roy White." To him, I looked like type of player who would do well in Japan. The Giants offered me a two-year contract worth $500,000. It was the biggest deal of my life.

I would be playing baseball after all in 1980 and 1981.

It was just going to be in Japan.

Chapter 12
Playing for the Yomiuri Giants
1980-1982

MY INTEREST IN JAPAN began when my sister Sonja toured there as a dancer as part of a Jenny Legong troupe, and she came back with great stories of the people and the culture. This happened back in the late 1950s when I was in middle school. She had been impressed with the country so much. Her stories fascinated me as someone interested in the world.

It was no surprise that my sister was a gifted dancer. Dance and other aspects of athleticism and entertainment had always been part of our lives growing up. My mom loved the theater and the arts. In fact, she wanted us to be entertainers. From the age of ten or eleven, I went to dance school. I had some tap, ballet, and afro jazz experience. I believe the dance training helped me as a ballplayer, especially as an outfielder. I believe that the dancing as a kid helped me become more athletic. Later on in life, my karate training also served a similar purpose, rounding me into the athlete I was.

With that as the background, a longtime interest in Japan and Japanese culture, and seeing an end to my Major League Baseball career in the United States, we made a deal with the Yomiuri Giants of Tokyo for me to continue my career, just in a different way and in a different place than I had originally envisioned at the time.

Today there are a lot of players who move from the United States to Japan and from Japan to the United States, but at the time I went to Japan, it wasn't as commonplace. This was 21 years before Ichiro Suzuki became a sensation in the USA.

Prior to me going, earlier in the 1970s, two of my former teammates on the Yankees, Clete Boyer and Joe Pepitone had gone to Japan to play, as had former American League MVP Zoilo Versalles and Willie Davis who had been an All-Star with the Dodgers. But, besides those players, there weren't too many other big-name players who made that journey.

I made the deal in December 1979. I would head to Japan in March. In preparation, I started to study the Japanese language.

Soon I was off to Japan, flying to Tokyo. The flight would be a long one, 15 hours. Because my children were in school, I had to leave my family behind. It would be months before I'd see them again. I'd be alone to start my new journey.

When the plane landed, the flight attendant told me that I had to stay aboard and would be the last one off. As I entered the airport terminal, there were hundreds of reporters gathered for an immediate press conference. I put on my new Tokyo Giants jersey, uniform #10. I also met my new interpreter, Ichiro "Ichi" Tanuma. The most popular question I was asked in that press conference was, "How many home runs will you hit?" I'd be asked that a lot in my years in Japan. I remember responding that I was a winning ballplayer. I didn't want to get into predictions like that. I wasn't even a home run hitter. It was all positive and celebratory. Japan seemed happy to have me. I was glad to be there.

Since I arrived in March (the Giants did not require me to attend the team's early camp), the rest of the team was at their Spring Training away from the city. Because of this, to begin my Japanese baseball career, I trained alone with just a coach in a village northwest of Tokyo called Tamagawa. There was a small baseball complex there with some fields. It was there that I exercised and went through the baseball drills—catching fly balls, throwing, and hitting. I did this for the first few weeks until my teammates arrived for the remainder of their training period which took place in Tokyo.

Much of my early time in Japan was spent at the baseball complex or alone. I would sometimes go into the city to go out to dinner but would return to the hotel when I realized I didn't know how to order food. Everything was different. My life was now a daily learning experience. Ichi would eventually take me to different places, and I started to try some different foods. I didn't like them all. I ate a lot of Ramen. Yakitori, a Japanese skewered chicken, also became a favorite.

For the first few weeks, I lived in a hotel until they found an apartment for me in the Hiroo Towers just outside Tokyo. This was an area of Japan with more foreigners which would also be good for my family when they arrived. While I was slowly acclimating to a new life, it was nice to be among people in similar situations to myself and some who were Americans as well.

During this period, I met Toru Shoriki, the owner of the Tokyo (Yomiuri) Giants. He gave me a pep talk. The Giants were, in many respects, the Yankees of Japan. He stated that they were very glad that I was in Japan and part of their team's storied history. I assured him that I would give the team my best.

It was around this time that I also learned the significance of my uniform number. Uniform number 10 was an important number for the Giants. For the previous four seasons it had been worn by Isao Harimoto, one of Japan's greatest players. Even today, all these years later, he remains the only player to amass more than 3,000 hits in Japan. He also still ranks as one of Japan's greatest home run hitters and was a great base stealer as well. Isao Harimoto is a legend in Japan. I learned quickly that "10" was a great number to have.

After a couple of weeks, I joined the team for the regular workouts. It was great meeting the other guys on the team. This included one of Japan's biggest baseball legends, their all-time home run king and now my teammate Sadaharu Oh, but he wasn't the only legend on the Giants.

Our manager, Shiego Nagashima, was also legendary as a player and as a manager. He was probably the most famous baseball player in Japan, even more than Sadaharu Oh and Isao Harimoto. Nagashima had been a great player and he was now a great manager. I knew it would be very special to play for him. I soon found that he liked the way I played the game and that he respected me as well.

It was nice to be treated like a top star. Playing for the Yomiuri Giants wasn't anything like what I experienced with the New York Yankees the previous three seasons. There was, as a part of the culture, a sense of respect between the players and the manager. There was a seriousness of purpose. In a way it was business-like, baseball is taken very seriously in Japan, but it was still baseball, and it was still fun.

The Japanese style of baseball incorporates a lot more training than in the USA. The manager deferred to my past history saying that I had been a member of the New York Yankees and a World Champion. Those facts earned me a lot of respect. In some of the training drills, they'd say, "You don't have to do this. You are a veteran and Yankee," but I did everything they did. This was their baseball. I was in Japan at their place. I wasn't going to impose my rules. I think, for those reasons, they liked me a lot. I didn't look for special treatment. I was just a member of the team looking to help us win games and maybe even the Japan Series (their version of America's World Series).

The Japanese definitely focused more on fundamentals and physical activity than their American counterparts. One example of this was what they called the One-Thousand Balls drill. It was exactly as it is called. Groundballs were hit to a player's left and right, over and over, and over again. This would take place for a long time, maybe an hour. In total, the player fielded a thousand balls (or close to it). The idea was for each player to be in his peak shape. That was essential. The Japanese prided themselves on physical fitness. They saw baseball as a very physical activity; one that required the players to always be at their best.

Physical activity in Japan was also used as a punishment. Rookies who forgot their gloves, for example, would have to run the stadium's stairs.

But then, on the other side, they also saw other things differently that went completely against my way of thinking and what I had been exposed to on teams all through my life including through all levels of professional baseball. In

America, players do not eat much before a game. In Japan, the players ate a four-course meal after batting practice and before each game. At first, I shied away from this, but soon I was right there with them, and I found that this didn't hinder my performance at all.

When I joined the Giants, there was a rule that a Japanese team couldn't have more than two former Major League players on their roster. The other American on the Giants in 1980 was John Sipin, a second baseman. In the United States, John had played for the San Diego Padres in 1969. He had been playing in Japan since 1971 and routinely hit .300 and powered out about 25 or more home runs a year. The 1980 season would end up being his last in Japan and in professional baseball. He was a great teammate. He gave me a lot of information about Japanese baseball and the customs. Since he had been in Japan for so long, he also spoke good Japanese. All of this was invaluable in my transition to this new culture.

Another person on the Giants who was very helpful was our hitting coach Wally Yonamine, another person with a fascinating history in sport. Yonamime was the first person of Japanese American descent to play in the National Football League when he played for the San Francisco 49ers in 1947. Later, he became the first American to play baseball professionally in Japan after World War II. In his baseball career, he won a few batting titles, was an All-Star often, won an MVP, and eventually made the Japanese Baseball Hall of Fame. Together, he and I often discussed hitting. He was a brilliant man. The knowledge he shared would serve me well in later years, after my playing days, when I became a coach myself.

I was very thankful for people like John Sipin and Wally Yonamine, and my Japanese teammates, who helped make my transition to Japanese baseball and Japanese life much easier.

In Japan, the preseason exhibition season is shorter. It was only six or seven games, but in that time I got a good sense of how the *shuuto*, a fastball that is so named because of its special movement, looks. A great Japanese pitcher Masahi Hiramatsu might have had the most famous *shuuto*. They called his pitch a razor *shuuto* because it seemed to cut the air when thrown. So much about the way the Japanese played baseball was different than in the USA. Even the pitches came to the batters in a different manner. In Japan, the pitchers threw variations on curve balls and sliders and other pitches. The movement on the ball as it approached home plate presented a different look than the way the ball comes at a batter in America. I knew I would have a lot to get used to.

I also learned that Japanese umpires sometimes called a bigger strike zone on the American batters. In that era, many Americans outperformed their Japanese counterparts. A bigger strike zone sometimes made things seem a little more equal. But it didn't feel so equal when they'd call strikes on me that they didn't call on other batters.

As the season came closer, I was still asked the same question time and again by the reporters, "How many home runs will you hit this year?" I still didn't have an answer. And I still didn't want to make any predictions in that department.

What I also couldn't predict was the hot start I got off to in Japan. Opening Day was in Yohohama against the Taiyo Whales. I was batting fourth in the lineup right after Sadaharu Oh. After hitting a popup in my first at bat, the next time I batted, I hit a huge home run—a rocket that went to the top of the stadium. I followed that with a double and then another home run in my next two at bats.

The Japanese soon started to tell me, "You have big power." It sure started out that way. For the first 15 or so games, I hit 6 or 7 home runs and was batting over .300. And then, I stopped getting the pitches. The Japanese pitchers learned how to pitch to me. I fell into a big slump.

In many regards, the Japanese methods were ahead of the American's. For example, some commonly used drills today such as hitting off tee and soft toss drills, were first practiced in Japan. But when it came to regular batting practice, they just threw the ball right down the middle so the batters would look great in that drill. This wasn't helping me as what I saw in BP was nothing like what I was facing in the games. I finally had to tell the guys throwing batting practice to pitch the ball away from me instead of right over the plate so I could find my swing and be productive in the games.

Most of the Japanese teams had one or two former Major Leaguers on their rosters. Getting to see the other Americans on the other teams was always fun. That year I saw Jim Lyttle who had played a few years with the Yankees (1969-71), along with Charlie Manuel, Leron Lee, Tommy Cruz, Tony Solaita, Steve Ontiveros, and others. After the games, we would meet up at a restaurant. These dinners were always a highlight. I would love talking with the American ballplayers. They would tell me stories about Japanese baseball. I learned a lot and it was great to have that connection to home. In the meantime, I was also learning the culture and language. It wasn't long before I had figured out the Japanese subway system.

It was easier to make time to meet after the games, because in Japan the games had a time limit. Japanese games were shorter, and they didn't go on forever as they sometimes do in America. The games in Japan began with a 6:00 p.m. start and were over by 8:30 p.m. It was a hard stop with the time limit that allowed the fans to take the trains and buses to get home since these did not run all night. In order to accommodate this time limit, the Japanese games were allowed to end in a tie.

Into June, I still wasn't hitting. It was a blessing when my wife and kids finally arrived.

My son Reade was eager to see me play in a game. I quickly took him to his first Japanese game at our home field, Korakuen Stadium, to see the Giants play the Hiroshima Carp. In my first at bat, in the first inning, batting left-handed, I homered. My next time up, I doubled. Later in the game, batting right-handed, I homered to tie the game and then in the 10th inning, I homered again to win it. I went 4-for-4 and was the game's hero. This was one of my greatest moments.

I told Reade that I'd be highlighted in the Japanese papers the next day, but it didn't quite come to be. Sadaharu Oh also homered in that game. It was his 756th lifetime home run which pushed his total past Hank Aaron for the most home runs in organized baseball on any continent. Oh's homer got most of the coverage. We had a good laugh about that. In my family, the player who got the biggest coverage was Reade. The Japanese dubbed him "Lucky Boy Reade."

Like that day back in 1968 when I held my crying daughter all night and then played the next day and never stopped hitting, bringing my son to the ballpark in Japan turned out to be good luck. From that point on, I did well in Japan. Reade's presence turned my career around. I have a lot to thank my kids for.

A short time after that big game, Sadaharu Oh invited us all out to dinner. Oh knew some English which was definitely a lot better than my Japanese. We met Oh at a Chinese restaurant, but as was custom, it was just him, not his family. Sadaharu had also ordered for us all and it included some interesting food choices—bear claw, shark fin soup, 100-year-old eggs. We politely ate what was put in front of us. It was a great night, but I wished my family would have had the chance to meet his.

During that time, I also had another star invite me out to dinner. Billy Joel reached out to me while he was on tour in Japan asking if I'd like to meet up for dinner after a game. I wasn't much into his music at the time, but I happily agreed, and we had a great time together. Billy Joel was a huge Yankees fan, and still is today.

There were certain aspects of Japanese baseball that were totally unlike anything I had experienced in America. One of those things was *kantoku shou*. We called this "Fighting Money." This was given out to the players if they did something great in a game, like a game-winning hit or a pitcher throwing a shutout. The manager kept track of how the players were doing and at the end of the month, if we did well, we'd get an envelope with extra cash on top of our salary. The better you did, the more extra money you made!

Another tradition I needed to get used to was the deference paid to veteran ballplayers. When a player came in from the field, a rookie would take his glove and hold it until the player needed to go back out.

The Japanese didn't have equipment managers. When a team went on the road, the players had to carry their own equipment and their clothing. No one had suitcases. The Japanese players knew how to pack light, getting all they needed into just a gym bag. I soon caught on.

I enjoyed these new traditions, expectations, and approaches to the game. From the start, I was welcomed and a real part of the team.

Once I established myself, I was moved from left field to centerfield where I played most of the year. I also found a permanent home in the number four spot in the batting order, clean up, right behind Sadaharu Oh. At the start of my career, I batted behind Mickey Mantle, one of America's greatest home run hitters, and now here I was batting behind Oh, Japan's greatest home run hitter. This was a tremendous honor.

By year's end, I had hit 29 home runs. Oh blasted 31 in what ended up being his last year as a player. He told me early on that this would be his last year so I knew that this would be a special year. Sadaharu Oh was a tremendous baseball player. Just seeing him in his last year made that very clear to me. I sometimes get asked by fans and sports writers if he would have been successful in the Major Leagues. There is no doubt that he would have done well. Sadaharu Oh hit the ball hard and he had legitimate power. He would be a baseball star anywhere.

One player I felt bad for that year was my new friend John Sipin. During the year, he struggled a bit with the bat. Prior to 1980, he was always a guy who batted around .300, but that year he hit only .224. He became a bench guy. I felt bad that I was playing every day and he wasn't. John Sipin was a really good guy, a friend who helped me acclimate to a new culture and find success in Japan. That season was his last as a professional baseball player.

The 1980 Yomiuri Giants finished in third place. That was a disappointment. Because of this, our manager, Shiego Nagashima stepped down. He felt it wasn't honorable to remain as the manager after doing this poorly. We had a very good team and while I didn't think it was our manager's fault that we didn't win the pennant, I felt we would have a great shot the next year. It was just like being with the Yankees in that respect. I was fortunate to play on a team comprised of players with exceptional talent.

With one season of Japanese baseball behind me, I looked forward to a few months back in the United States. Still, overall, it was a great experience living and traveling throughout Japan. I learned a great deal, as did my family. The Japanese culture was so different. In many ways it was a very respectful society. It was also very safe. We felt comfortable going anywhere. In a way, even though we were on a different continent and in a completely different culture, we felt at home.

In regard to technology, the Japanese had things that were way ahead of the USA. I remember the big video games like Space Invaders and Donkey Kong. Japan had them way before they came to America. They also had Sony Walkmans, electronic Casio watches, GameBoys, and so much more. There was a shopping area known as Akihabara or "Electronics Town." They had all of the new technological items. We loved shopping there and seeing things we had never even imagined. We'd bring back items, like the Casio watches, that amazed our friends at home.

My second season in Japan came quickly. There were some big changes. First, we had our new manager, Motoshi Fujita. Fujita had been a star pitcher in Japan in the 1960s and had served as Yomiuri's pitching coach when they had won nine consecutive Japan Series in the 1970s. He was well-respected. My teammate from the previous season, the great Sadaharu Oh, moved on to be the team's assistant manager. And, after helping me so much in my first season, John Sipin had returned to the United States and retired from baseball. Taking his place on the team was a former teammate of mine from my Yankees days, Gary Thomasson.

It was great to be able to play the role of mentor for Gary. We had been teammates on the Yankees in 1978 and 1979. He was a really nice guy. This was now my chance to teach someone the ropes and the customs. We had a good relationship over there.

As part of our Spring Training in 1981, the Yomiuri Giants actually went to Vero Beach, Florida and trained for a while with the Los Angeles Dodgers. I remember my old friend and teammate from home, Reggie Smith, asking me all about playing in Japan. He was getting friendly with the Giants' general manager. The idea of playing there piqued his interest as his own Major League career was winding down. This would play out in an interesting way for both of us.

We played a few exhibition games in Florida that year. I recall playing the Dodgers, of course, and also the Texas Rangers. We played well and won a couple of the games. Back then, and still maybe even today, there was a perception that the American ballplayers were so much better than the Japanese players. That just wasn't true. There were a bunch of guys I played with and against in Japan who would have been solid major leaguers. Sadaharu Oh could have played and been a star anywhere. But he wasn't the only one. On the Giants, we had a starting pitcher named Suguru Egawa. He threw hard. He went 55-30 in the years I was with Yomiuri. We also had Mitsuo Sumi a top relief pitcher who would have been an ace closer in the United States. He had a slider that was just unhittable. The Taiyo Whales had a relief pitcher named Kazuhiko Endo. I couldn't hit him. He struck me out the first five times I faced him. And there were many others. Suffice to say, the Japanese had their fair share of outstanding ballplayers. I think it's great today when we can see the talented players from Japan come to the Major Leagues and be big stars. Guys like Ichiro Suzuki, Hideki Matsui, Hideo Nomo, Yu Darvish, Masahiro Tanaka, and so many others, are now considered greats on two continents.

That second season went very well for us. I had a solid season, not quite as good as my first, but I still batted .273 with 13 homers. Gary Thomasson hit 20 homers. We also had a rookie, Tatsunori Hara, who would go on to be a Japanese star, who led the team in homers with 22.

We won the pennant with a 73-48-9 record and played the Nippon-Ham Fighters in the Japan Series. This was an interesting series since all the games were played in Tokyo at Korakuen Stadium which was the home park for both teams.

We lost the first game, but in the 8th inning of the second

game, I blasted a big home run that turned out to be the game winner as we won 2-1. This also seemed to be the turning point of the series as we won three of the next four games to win the championship. My team was, once again, at the top of the baseball world in its country. It felt great, almost the same as with the Yankees. An interesting fact is that I was the first player to ever win a World Series with the Yankees and a Japan Series with the Giants, the best baseball team in each country. Since then, one other player has also done this, Hideki Matsui. He first won in Japan and then with the 2009 Yankees. We were both also left fielders. Before he came to the Yankees and the Major Leagues, I scouted Hideki Matsui. But that's a story for later.

After two successful seasons, and a championship now under my belt, I signed a new contract for a third season in Japan. Gary Thomasson also came back. I hit .296 that third year. I felt I still had a lot more in the tank. Things were going well for me in Japan, and I enjoyed it there. Our team finished in second place just a half game out at season's end. The way that season concluded became famous in Japanese baseball.

We needed the Chunichi Dragons to lose the last game for us to win the pennant. The Dragons were playing the Taiyo Whales. Both teams had a player going for the batting title. Yasushi Tao of the Dragons (who hit .350) walked four times in the game and scored a bunch of runs to lead the Dragons to victory which knocked us out. Keiji Nagasaki of Taiyo, who wasn't walked each time he came to the plate, ended up winning the batting title with a .351 average.

I had three hits my last game in Japan that 1982 season. My interpreter said they'd contact me if they wanted to sign me again. I hit close to .300 my last season. I was still in good shape, and I felt good. I still wanted to play baseball and I felt that I had a season or two left in me. I was 38 years old, but I didn't feel that I was done yet.

It turned out that I was done.

Ichi Tanuma, my interpreter, called me and said that the Giants would be moving on from me. It turns out they signed a different player from the United States. They signed Reggie

Smith, my friend and competitor from Compton. My baseball playing days were over.

Playing Baseball in Japan with Roy White

By John Sipin

John Sipin and Roy White were teammates on the Yomiuri Giants in Japan for one season, 1980. Sipin had played Major League Baseball with the San Diego Padres in 1969 before beginning his career in Japan in 1972. In Japan, Sipin was a star. In his nine seasons in Japan, Sipin played with the Taiyo Whales and Yomiuri Giants. He hit over .300 six times and hit over 20 home runs in a season seven times.

***

I N 1980, I HAD the pleasure of playing alongside Roy White on the Yomiuri Giants. Roy was a true American baseball star. I was thrilled to be his teammate. I don't do a lot of interviews. The reason why I agreed to this is because of who Roy White is. I enjoyed every moment with him. I was glad that I had so much experience as an American ballplayer in Japan that I could assist Roy as he acclimated to baseball in that country.

Playing baseball in Japan was a unique experience. Baseball in Japan the 1970s was a lot different than it is today and it was much different than baseball in America. While the rules of the game were basically the same on the two continents, the traditions, the expectations, and the way the players and teams trained were extremely unalike.

In America, I was originally drafted and signed by the St. Louis Cardinals organization. That was in 1965. I worked my way through the minor leagues and reached Triple-A by 1969.

In that season I was traded to the San Diego Padres and made my Major League debut with them that year. My debut came against Chicago Cubs lefty Ken Holtzman. I hit back-to-back triples on my first two big league at bats. These each came on the first pitches thrown to me. This is still a major league record!

I played one season for the Padres as a second baseman. I then spent the 1970 (Salt Lake City) and 1971 (Hawaii) seasons at Triple-A hitting over .300 both seasons. I knew I was ready for the big leagues, but the Padres were slow to promote me.

Former Yankee, Clete Boyer, who had been a teammate of Roy White's when he first came up, was an American player who had decided to play in Japan for the 1972 season. We had played together in Hawaii in 1971. Boyer reached out to me knowing that the Padres planned for me to spend another year in the minor leagues and let me know that his team, the Taiyo Whales, had an opening for one more American player. At the time, each Japanese team was permitted to have two American players on their roster. The decision between playing in the big leagues in Japan or the minor leagues in America was an easy one for me. I decided to go to Japan.

Clete and I played together for four seasons, 1972-75. We both found success in Japan. Clete was finishing his career, but for me, mine was just beginning in many ways. I was just 25 years old.

The Japanese baseball season was only 130 games, as compared to 162 games in the USA. I was hitting around .300 most seasons and clubbing twenty to thirty home runs. It was great to find this level of success in Japan. I loved playing there and acclimated well to their culture and style of play.

After the 1975 season, while there were Americans on my teams for three years, they were released, and I was the only foreigner. Of course, none was of the stature of Roy White, a New York Yankee, an All-Star, and a World Champion. I was so excited when Roy came to join the Yomiuri Giants as my teammate for the 1980 season (I had joined the Giants, widely considered the Yankees of Japan in 1978). I always found it interesting that the two biggest stars I played with in Japan had both been New York Yankees, and they had both worn uniform #6.

The game in Japan is a different game. One big difference was the time limit for the games. For example, an inning cannot begin after a three-hour time limit. Teams must, of course, finish that inning, but once it's over, the game ends. This results in different strategies being used as the game gets close to the time limit. Games in Japan also, because of this, can end in ties.

The Japanese were also very opinionated. They seemed to scrutinize everything. They had a way of either praising you or silencing you out. It was important to understand all of this so that you knew what's going on. The only year I played with Roy White, I had challenges. My season began slowly, I wasn't hitting. I knew I'd come around, but the Japanese have a way of shutting you down. They don't always give second chances—even to an established player like me. By the time Roy and I were teammates, I was in my ninth season in Japan. Pitchers on the other teams started throwing at my head. I soon found myself benched.

Still, being a teammate with Roy White was a privilege. Roy was a gentleman. He was always kind. He never lost his cool. He took immediately to the Japanese culture and the expectations. In the beginning, the Japanese players deferred to Roy White saying he didn't have to do some of the more rigorous drills, but Roy showed what a person and teammate he is by doing everything expected of all the players.

Roy was more than an athlete as well. He's a smart person. He always had a book with him. He is an avid reader. His son, too.

When Roy came, I became his mentor, teaching him all about Japan and Japanese baseball. I had a car so I could serve as his chauffer. I could speak Japanese well enough; I knew my way around. Coming over to Japan without someone to help could be intimidating—a person could be lost. I was glad that I could be the guide and the friend to Roy White.

I helped Roy find his apartment in the Hiroo Towers—a

great area in Tokyo. I showed Roy my favorite places to eat. We talked a lot. It was great.

Japan at that time was a special place. You never locked your doors. If you left something on the train, they'd deliver it back to you. There was great respect. People just did not take what wasn't theirs. There were not many foreigners in Japan when we were there. Many Japanese also didn't speak English. We had interpreters, but they didn't always tell us everything. I was never going to put Roy in a bad situation.

Roy was very observant. He didn't always say a lot. Instead, he observed. He took a lot in with his eyes. He watched and he learned. He was always respectful, and he was always a professional. He was perfect. A lot of players go to Japan and want to play American baseball there. That doesn't work. You don't mess with Japanese baseball. Roy played Japanese baseball the Japanese way.

The Japanese trained hard. We'd be out on the field for eight hours. Groundball practice would last for an hour at a time. The team would use four different batters to hit the fungos at you, each would work in fifteen-minute shifts. That was tough. They would wear you out. The Japanese never want to lose a game for lack of training as an excuse for poor performance. In America, we reviewed plays, maybe ran through them a few times in Spring Training. In Japan that doesn't exist. You might go over a play 100 times, maybe 1,000 times. They would break the body to build the spirt. They wanted to know how much you could take.

The weather, also, was not great. Spring Training was cold and dry. Our bats would literally dry out and shatter in our hands. During the summer, the heat and humidity is oppressive. Japanese baseball takes a lot to get used to, but Roy White just acclimated to it all. They loved him in Japan. Still do.

During the games, the fans had all sorts of chants. They are big on vocal and visual noise. They had plastic things that they would bang on all game. The stands were always packed. The Giants sold out every game at home and on the road. If you enjoyed hitting in pressure, they were the team to play for. Roy White thrived in that environment.

With Yomiuri, we both got to play with the great Sadaharu Oh. He was unbelievable. I played against him for six years and with him for three. He wasn't just a great ballplayer, he was an amazing athlete. He won back-to-back Triple Crowns and became the all-time home run king. He also walked about 120 times a year, even with the shorter schedule. Oh was one of a kind. Some people wonder if he could have played in the Major Leagues. He could. Easily. He'd have been a star in America.

A lot of the Japanese players I saw would have made it in the USA. Shigeo Nagashima was known as the "Golden Boy" and "Mr. Japanese Baseball." He became a legend when he hit three homers in an All-Star Game when the Emperor of Japan was in attendance. He is considered by many to be the greatest Japanese player of all-time. He and Sadaharu Oh joined to lead the Giants to nine consecutive Japan Series victories. Amazing.

Later, he was the manager of the Giants who traded for me.

After that 1980 season. I came home. I was mentally tired. Billy Martin and Clete Boyer offered me to get in shape and play second base for the Oakland A's, but I was tired of traveling and knew I didn't want to be away from my wife, and I was ready to start a family. Charlie Metro, who I knew from the St. Louis Cardinals organization, offered me the chance to manage the A's Triple-A club. I also turned him down.

I've been living in Santa Cruz, California since then and been invited to Japan for Legends and Hall of Fame games—one was with Roy. I've been back to Japan 20 or so times, bringing my family and having my girls, who turned out to be outstanding athletes, meet Nagashima and Oh and all my Japanese friends. I loved Japan and I was glad to have my final season there with Roy White as my teammate.

Chapter 13
Now a Coach
1983-1984

THE WINTER BEFORE THE 1983 season had me itching to play baseball again. The Yankees contacted me and inquired about me being a coach. I wasn't so sure about that. I still saw myself as a player. I was hoping for an offer from a team. I had just batted close to .300 in Japan. I knew I could still play.

I talked a lot about this with Murray Bauer, my best friend, and the person who now runs the Roy White Foundation. I had known Murray for many years. Murray was a person I knew I could trust. I always valued his advice (and still do). In this, he advised that I needed to go out as a New York Yankee and not as a member of any other team. He said, "You could play with a team like the Royals, and it would be great, but it would look better in the end if you just played with the Yankees in the United States and the Giants in Japan, the two best teams." This made a lot of sense. What also helped with my decision was the very critical fact that I also wasn't getting any offers to play.

In retrospect, I have very few regrets. I wasn't a player who looked at statistics, I just went out and played my best baseball year-after-year. I worked hard. I stayed in shape. I tried to be a great teammate and a winner. And I worked to set a good example for the younger players, and really all the players. I took my job as a baseball player very seriously. I gave it my all. When it was over, and I looked back, I did notice a few things. My career ended with some totals that were just short of a few significant round numbers.

In my Major League career, I ended with 1,803 hits. One more good season, or so, and I would have had 2,000. Likewise, with home runs. I was a little farther off there, ending with 160, but if one were to add my Japanese totals to the MLB totals, it all looks a bit better. Including my three years in Japan, I had 2,152 hits and 214 homers to go along with 930 runs batted in. (Even with the Japan numbers, I was a full year short of another big round number there. One thousand RBI's would have been nice.)

Murray Bauer, though, was correct. Ending my playing career with the Yankees was the right thing to do. Murray is a friend but also my biggest fan. He points out that as a Yankee, I ended up alongside some of the all-time greats. When I retired, I was fifth all-time on the Yankees in games played. I was also in the top ten in hits, runs scored, walks, stolen bases, and doubles. I wasn't a power hitter, and always when I thought I might be one and tried to hit the ball out of the park, I'd find myself in a slump, but even with that, I was in the top 15 all-time in home runs and runs batted in as a Yankee.

It was a career I am very proud of. I may have wanted it to last a bit longer, but when I do look back, I do so with a great deal of satisfaction.

With the 1983 Yankees, I would be the first base coach. Billy Martin was the manager. I knew I would learn a lot about baseball watching Billy's mind work now as a coach and not as a player. Don Zimmer, who had managed the 1978 Red Sox, was also on the coaching staff as was Yogi Berra, among others. At 39-years-old, I was the youngest coach on the team. Jeff Torborg, who was 41, was the closest in age to me.

In many ways, I felt awkward as a coach. I felt I was too young, and I still wanted to play. At one point I told Billy Martin that I could still play the outfield. "I'm in good shape," I told him. In Spring Training, I even took some batting practice, but Billy laughed it off. I honestly didn't see what was so funny. Lou Piniella, who was a friend and teammate, from 1974 through 1979 was my same age and he was still playing. But it wasn't to be.

I soon learned that you didn't do much coaching when you

worked with Billy Martin. He ran the show. Completely. There wasn't a lot of input to give, and further, I just wasn't that close to him. I didn't join Billy's clique, the group of coaches led by Art Fowler, who went out with him frequenting the bars on most nights. That wasn't my style as a player, and it wasn't going to be my style as a coach.

I remember doing my job standing in the first base coach's box watching the game action and wishing, desperately, that I was the guy batting or running the bases. Playing baseball had been part of my whole life. From hitting rocks in my driveway pretending I was a big leaguer, to playing sock ball with friends, and then Little League, American Legion, high school, and all the way up, I worked diligently to realize my dream of being a big league ballplayer. And I made it and did well. In some ways, it was all I knew. To be on the field but removed from the action and not playing was hard. It was a difficult transition for me.

Old feelings die hard, but they eventually go away. I remember standing as a coach the next year and watching Dave Steib of the Toronto Blue Jays pitching. He was working on a great game. He might have allowed only one hit or so. I recall watching Dave Winfield struggling against this masterful pitcher. At that moment I thought to myself, "I'm glad I'm not playing."

But now I was a coach. Once I settled into the role, it was a special experience. The 1983 Yankees was a team with a great collection of exceptional ballplayers. One of those players was the rookie, Don Mattingly. When one is a first base coach, that is not the extent of his responsibilities. I worked with the hitters, the outfielders, and also taught some base running. With Don Mattingly, I was able to work with him on his hitting. I showed him a few things. Don Mattingly enjoyed talking hitting as did I. I was amazed how hard he worked. He never took the easy way out. He went through all the drills, hard. Don Mattingly never gave himself a break. We went at it one hundred percent, always. In a way, this reminded me of Mickey Mantle who also never took the easy way out. Mickey and Don played the game with enthusiasm, seriousness, and a strong desire to always be their best and to win. It was too bad that Mattingly never had the chance to experience a World Championship in New York as a player.

Dave Winfield was another great athlete and player on that team. Winfield was six feet, six inches. Often players that tall aren't able to do some of the necessary baseball movements, but Winfield could. He played outfield as well as anyone. Like me, he'd often leap over the wall to rob an opposing player of a home run. Unlike me, Dave Winfield had one of the strongest arms of any player ever. That man threw laser beams.

In 1984, Rickey Henderson was brought to New York in a trade. Incredible is the only word to describe Rickey Henderson. This was a man with such amazing athleticism. He was a ball of muscle and was so fast and agile. He could run at full speed and make a 90-degree left-hand turn. I've never seen anyone else who could do that. I taught base running and how to steal bases, but I didn't talk to Rickey about those things. There was no need. He was the best ever.

Another hard-working player was a kid who was a rookie in 1984, Mike Pagliarulo. I couldn't get "Pags" out of the batting cage. Like Mattingly, he had this innate drive to push himself to be his best. I worked with Pagliarulo a lot. He was so motivated, I was afraid (also like Mattingly) that he could overdo it. I finally told him that he'd only get 100 swings, no more. But then I'd arrive at the ballpark and find him hitting. He was wound up tight. My favorite phrase to Pags was "relax."

The 1983 and 1984 Yankees were very good. The tough part was we were just close, but just not quite good enough. In 1983, the team won 91 games, but we only came in third place. We came in third in 1984 as well with 87 wins. If we only had a little more pitching, things could have been different.

One difference, also, between those two years was in the way the team was managed. After the 1983 season, Billy Martin was let go. The manager in 1984 was Yogi Berra. That year, 1984, Lou Piniella joined me on the coaching staff. Lou would eventually become a great manager himself, but we never saw him in that role when he played. It goes to show that one never knows a person's future.

In 1984, with Yogi at the helm, the overall atmosphere was a lot calmer. When Billy Martin managed a team, that team always played well. Billy's success cannot be denied. But he did it in a way that had the players on edge. Yogi, like Bob Lemon in 1978, had a different approach. It was more laid back. Billy told everyone what to do. Yogi trusted the players more. In their own ways, they were both very good managers. A manager has to be true to himself. He can't manage someone else's way. Billy, Yogi, Bill Virdon, Bob Lemon, Ralph Houk, Motoshi Fujita, and Shiego Nagashima were all very successful managers. Joe Torre too. I was fortunate to play or work with all of them.

We didn't have an official batting coach in those years. I just kind of assumed the role and did it. I liked hitting, talking about hitting, and figuring out what it takes to be a great hitter. When I played, we also didn't have a batting coach. Instead, different coaches at different times would offer advice. Dick Howser and Ellie Howard were two coaches who helped me with my hitting. Bill Virdon, when he was the manager, also took an interest in the batters and offered sage advice. Of course, in those days, we also weren't into video much. That started coming in the 1980s with the players looking at their swings in the video room. We did it more organically. We'd work side-by-side with a player and break his swing down to find out how he could be at his best.

I believe the first coaches to be exclusive batting coaches were Charlie Lau with the Royals and Walt Hriniak of the Red Sox. With the Yankees, especially the year Lou Piniella and I coached together, we'd just work with certain players to get the job done. I'd like to think that we were pretty successful.

It was a team effort. As Yankees coaches, we had a job to do. The goal was to get the Yankees to the playoffs and the World Series. It was disappointing that that didn't happen those first years I was a coach.

After the 1984 season, the Yankees went a different direction, and my coaching career came to a close. I'd be back on the field again one day again as a coach, I just didn't know that at the time.

Chapter 14
The Front Office
1985

MY FIRST STINT AS a Yankees coach ended after the 1984 season. I was soon asked to move to the front office and serve as the assistant to Clyde King, the Yankees General Manager.

A few years previous, I was a baseball player. Within three years of the end of my playing days, I now found myself among the decision-makers far removed from the game on the field itself.

My responsibilities in this regard were multifaceted. There was front office work to do, but I was also assigned to work with the various teams in the Yankees system, so I would still be close to the game itself, at least on occasion.

I was involved as an executive in meetings, some not so pleasant such as when Yogi Berra's tenure and his association with the Yankees ended shortly into the 1985 season. That decision was made around a big conference table with many important people present including George Steinbrenner, Clyde King, and of course Yogi. I was present at that table, but, this isn't my story to share. I believe that some things are best left behind closed doors. I will say this, it wasn't a pleasant or happy meeting. Once Yogi walked out the door of that conference room, he didn't return to the Yankees in any capacity, for fifteen long years. Yogi only returned to the Yankees after George Steinbrenner went to his museum at Montclair University and publicly apologized to Yogi.

I remember another executive-level meeting that involved personnel. This meeting had to have been in 1986, during Spring Training where I was serving as an instructor. Even when players weren't coaching specifically with the organization, the Yankees would invite former players to Spring Training to assist with getting the players ready. In 1986, Lou Piniella was the Yankees manager. He'd replaced Billy Martin who had been brought in for the third time to replace Yogi Berra after he'd walked out that conference room door.

I remember Pete Sheehey looking for me and finding me in the shower after a game. He said, "Roy, they need you." George Steinbrenner's office was in a trailer, but it still had a big conference table in there. I walked in to find the whole coaching staff and front office there all seated around this big table. There was one seat left, right next to George. He looked right at me and said, "Roy, we have to cut one of the pitchers. It's either Phil Niekro or Tommy John. The vote is tied." This was a tough call. Both of these pitchers had been great, but they were both well over 40-years-old. Still, I felt both had a little something left in the tank. I voted to keep Phil Niekro. The room went silent. That wasn't the answer Steinbrenner wanted. Finally, everyone looked at George. He said, "I didn't vote yet. I vote for Tommy John and my vote counts twice."

In my front office capacity, I was also involved in scouting, evaluating minor leaguers, especially the Triple-A team in Columbus (but I was able to see all the minor league teams and players), and evaluating talent from other clubs for potential trades. My role was multifaceted. Best of all, I was also used as a roving instructor throughout the minor leagues.

One player I remember scouting quite a bit was Darrell Evans, a left-handed third and first baseman with power. The Yankees were interested in him because even though he was aging (he was 38 years old in 1985) he still possessed a great home run swing that could have fit Yankee Stadium very well. And, as it turned out, he led the American League in home runs that year with 40. He then hit 29 in 1986 and 34 in 1987. I thought Evans would have been a great fit for those Yankees teams, but the deal just couldn't be worked out.

I especially enjoyed working with the Yankees' minor leaguers. The Yankees had a bunch of good guys down there who I worked with—players who would go on to have pretty good careers. One of these players was Roberto Kelly. I worked with Roberto a lot, I even tried to make him a switch hitter, but that experiment didn't last.

Another player I worked with was Jim Leyritz. His idol growing up was Pete Rose and like Rose, he worked hard and played hard. Leyritz didn't possess a ton of talent, but he had great determination and focus. He could actually hit left-handed pretty well, so I also worked with him at being a switch hitter, just like his idol Pete Rose, but as a professional, Leyritz stayed as a right-handed hitter. In the 1990s, he would hit a few memorable postseason home runs to help the Yankees achieve glory once again.

When I was in New York, I'd often be at the stadium and watch the games with Clyde King from the owner's suite. Of course, there were times when George Steinbrenner would sit in with us as well. Let's just say that it was always better in the box with George when the Yankees were winning.

I enjoyed the position as Assistant to the General Manager. It kept me in the game, and I saw the business side of baseball and even the game itself from a new perspective.

The 1985 Yankees were a very good club. They won 97 games that year but still finished in second place. In the 1980s, there were no expanded playoffs. It was first place or nothing. And, for the Yankees, and George Steinbrenner, second place was the same as saying "first loser." Unfortunately, year-after-year, that's just where the Yankees seemed to finish. They were close, but just not quite good enough. I was reminded of the 1970 Yankees and the 1974 team as well. It is frustrating as a player, coach, or executive to be that close, to be very good, but not quite good enough.

I sometimes wonder how Yankees history would have changed if the expanded playoffs of today had been in existence those years. The Yankees would have qualified for the playoffs each of those years and in a short series anything could have happened. It's likely there would have been a World Championship or two, but it wasn't to be. Not then.

In those years, there was also constant change. Clyde King

would be out as the General Manager after the 1986 season. Lou Piniella too. Although, in 1988, Piniella returned as manager after Billy Martin's fourth tour of duty in that role.

For me, my position as an executive with the Yankees lasted just one season.

I soon found myself, for the first time in my life, out of baseball.

What Roy White Means to the Yankees
by Ray Negron

Bronx native Ray Negron became a Yankees bat boy and team executive. He has been with the Yankees for close to fifty years. In his quiet way, he has seen it all in that time. His perspective on the Yankees as a team and all of the players is unique and always honest.

***

I **HAVE BEEN IN** baseball for close to fifty years, but I have been a fan even longer. Throughout that time, I have watched, admired, looked up to, and even worked with Roy White. In short, he was always, always, the classiest guy on the field, in the clubhouse, or in the executive meeting room. He is one of the most respected guys in the game. He is a living Yankees legend. A true special person. And the Yankees leadership today doesn't even know what they have there. Why Roy White isn't in Monument Park is something that needs to be corrected—immediately.

I grew up in the Bronx, a true inner-city kid. Many people know my story. I was a big Yankees fan as a kid growing up in the 1960s. Like so many kids in the neighborhood, Roy White was my hero. In the early 1970s, I was caught spray painting graffiti on the outside walls of Yankee Stadium, but instead of getting me punished, George Steinbrenner saw something in me and brought me in to work in the clubhouse as a Yankees bat boy. Because of this, I got to see my hero up close. So often when we meet the people we look up to, we get disappointed. Too many heroes have clay feet. Not Roy White. He was a true human being, a great man, a welcomer. People use the word "class." That sums it up. Roy was all "class."

Where I grew up, minority kids, including Blacks and Hispanics, needed someone to look up to, one of our own to root for. The Yankees legends from the previous decade, guys like Elston Howard (and Mickey Mantle and Whitey Ford) had left the team. We needed a hero. People might forget now, but racism was a part of it all then. This was the Civil Rights era. Rev. Dr. Martin Luther King was assassinated. Robert Kennedy too. We needed a hero. And that hero became Roy White.

Roy was a person who was above it all. He wore an afro like so many of us. He was himself. He didn't get distracted by the negativity. Instead, he just did his job. He played the game hard. He was always there. He was rock-solid and couldn't be rattled. He was someone to look up to. And we did. All of us. And he never let us down because of the dignity with which he carried himself.

When the Yankees were so bad, he was so good. He kept our interest. Roy White was the player who helped keep the franchise afloat.

He never got the credit or the recognition for that. And he was never a self-promoter. If the Yankees just step back a bit, they'd see this. The fact that they haven't is upsetting. It's wrong.

***

As I shared, when I became a bat boy, Roy White was that same person off the field and out of the spotlight (not that he ever craved the spotlight). He was always the classiest guy in the clubhouse. He was always one of the top most respected guys in there. It was Roy White and Thurman Munson who were the players everyone looked up to. And people don't know this, but I do, Thurman Munson also looked up to Roy White. I saw this every single day. And they talked every day since their lockers were right next to each other.

People have asked if Roy White went out of his way to welcome me to the team. The answer to that might surprise some. No, he didn't. Roy White didn't go out of his way to be welcoming and supportive. He didn't go out of his way to do that. It *was* his way. Being kind was just a natural thing for Roy White. He didn't go out of his way to be nice. He was just nice. With Roy you knew what you got. That's who Roy White was. It's who he still is today.

Roy was a no-nonsense type of guy. What you saw was what you got. When I looked at Roy White in that era I thought, "This is what it must have been like to see Lou Gehrig when he played." I've been with the Yankees a long time. Back in the 1970s, I got to know many of the players that played with Gehrig. I also became close with Mrs. Eleanor Gehrig. I asked them all if they saw what I saw, that Roy White was the Lou Gehrig of his era. And, after thinking about it, they all agreed. There was so much about them that was the same—the fact that they always played, the fact that they always gave their best, and the fact that they would be described as dignified. I remember asking that of Pete Sheehey, the longtime clubhouse attendant who began his work in the days of Babe Ruth and Lou Gehrig. Pete said to me, "You know, now that you say it, I wouldn't say that you're wrong."

Think about that for a moment. That was Roy White. Roy White was, in many ways, the Lou Gehrig of the Yankees. Everyone looked up to Roy. He was Old Reliable. There was nothing that Roy couldn't do. He could hit for average. He could hit the ball out when needed. Roy was the Yankees' clean-up hitter for many years. He protected Mickey Mantle and Bobby Murcer who batted third, just as Lou Gehrig protected Babe Ruth. He could run. He played great defense. Who doesn't remember Roy White leaping into the stands to rob a player of a home run? In the clutch, in a big game, if Thurman Munson didn't come through, we knew that Roy would and vice versa.

It's fun to remember all this. The batboys "dug" Roy. This was the era of Bruce Lee and Roy was a martial artist. He was very good at it. He knew the moves and would display them in the clubhouse. There was a big song in that era called "Kung Fu Fighting." Roy would make the moves according to the song. We'd just watch. We were looking for someone to look up to.

Roy didn't really understand that. He was just being himself. He didn't realize how much we looked up to him. We grew our hair like Roy White.

The Yankees started winning in the late 1970s and Roy White was a big part of that. He was the bridge between Mickey Mantle and Reggie Jackson. I don't think the Yankees would have been as good as they were without Roy White. He was that important to the team.

***

In later years, I got to see Roy after his career as a coach. He was great at that. There are certain coaches who have credibility and stature that the players listen to them. That was Roy White. He was so good in that role. He knew how to teach. And he knew so much about the game, he was such a student of the game, that the suggestions, the lessons, and the advice he gave, was taken to heart by the players. Roy White had that kind of stature and respect.

I also saw and worked with Roy the year he was in the front office. I didn't like seeing Roy White in a suit. He cares so much about the players as people and their livelihoods that the cut-throat aspects of upper baseball management didn't fit him as much. Roy wasn't that kind of person. He cared too much. Those kinds of decisions were difficult. Roy White was more qualified to be on the field. He's a builder of people, not someone who tears them down. He finds places for people, he's not the type to take their jobs away from them.

***

Lou Gehrig was overshadowed by Babe Ruth and later Joe DiMaggio. When he played, he wasn't respected the way he was after he got sick.

Roy White is, and has been, overlooked in many ways. Too many ways. The Yankees have this wonderful thing called Monument Park. It's where they recognize the greats in their history. Roy White belongs there. He deserves to be there. It has always made me sad for Roy. I know he won't say it, but I know it bothers him.

So many players are recognized there, or have their number retired, who weren't half the player or person Roy White was. Just from the standpoint of being a decent human being. Roy White wore the Yankees uniform for 15 years. He never made them look bad. He always represented the Yankees very well. Always. The Yankees don't know what they have in Roy White. I can't explain it. They don't understand what he meant to the team. They also don't understand what he meant to the community during the civil rights years, and beyond, and how he represented us all so wonderfully.

I like to introduce him as "The real #6... Roy White." I say that with all due respect to Joe Torre, who the number is retired for. But it should have been retired for Roy White years before.

Roy White is a Yankee treasure.

He belongs in Monument Park.

Chapter 15
In and Out of Baseball
1986-2005

FOR ALL INTENTS AND purposes, my life had revolved around baseball, first as a player, then as a coach and executive. The entirety of my adult life centered around the game. But now I was in my early forties, and I had to find a new career. I wasn't sure if I'd ever get the call to be a coach or an executive again. It was time to seriously consider my new life—my life out of the game.

In most professions, people find a career path and work in that occupation in various capacities for many years until they retire. Retirement usually comes in one's fifties or sixties. It's not that way in sports. We are forced to recognize our mortality, if you will, much earlier. Our careers end when we are far too young. We go from being immortals, some might even call us heroes, to becoming everyday people far too quickly. One day you're on top of the world, and the next, well, you're left wondering what's next.

My life out of baseball took a number of different paths— all good, just different. I valued and made the most of each experience. One thing I am good at is making the most out of every day.

My separation from the game, I'm not sure it was really a "retirement," brought about a lot more time for me to spend with my family. That was one very big bonus. Professional athletes do not get to have much family time as we train, travel, and play. I loved being a professional baseball player, but it does come at a cost. In order for a person to be at the top of his game, he has to invest a ton of time at his craft. On any team, there is always another player, often younger, faster, or stronger, that wants to take your job. In order to stay at the top, a player must be all-in. It is a relentless pursuit to be one's best and to be at the top of one's game. I did that for over twenty years as a professional baseball player. Working as a coach and an executive is a year-round job in many ways. There are always decisions that have to be made. There's always another team looking to get an edge. After so much time away, I was glad to have time to focus on my wife and children. That time was invaluable to me.

One new profession I pursued was an extension of a hobby that I, and many of the Yankees had enjoyed—racehorses. As a player, I would often go to the track to watch and bet on the horses at the various tracks around the country. As we traveled from city to city, there was a lot of down time between the games. Watching the ponies helped fill up some of that time. I used to enjoy going to the track with Lou Piniella, Mickey Rivers, Don Gullett, and others. A number of times Howard Cosell would meet up with us at the track. We had a lot of laughs. We never bet a lot of money, nor did we win a lot, but it was a lot of fun. Yankees owner George Steinbrenner also loved the races and owned a few horses himself. As professional ballplayers, baseball also wasn't ever far from our minds. Even at the track, among teammates, we'd talk baseball and strategy. I believe this was one reason the Yankees at that time were so good. We had fun, we enjoyed each other's company, but we were also serious about the game, even in down times.

After I left the game, I was offered the opportunity to join in a partnership in Major League Standardbreds to invest in some harness race horses. In these deals there would usually be about ten investors who might each contribute about fifteen hundred dollars in a racehorse. If that horse won, we'd get a percentage of the prize money. This was fun and I was provided a behind-the-scenes look at the horse racing profession. I created the name of the company and Reade drew up the logo. Like baseball, and everything else, there is so much that happens before the races, in training, regarding nutrition, and so much more, that the viewing public never gets to see or even know. In some ways, regarding the preparation and all that goes into winning, including the singular focus on working to be one's best, horse racing wasn't all that different from being a professional baseball player.

I invested in a number of horses, but the best of them, by far, was a mare named Saccharum. She became a champion and was so fast, she often defeated the male horses. I watched her race at the Meadowlands and at Yonkers. She was trained by Jerry Silverman who was an exceptional trainer and is now in the Harness Racing Museum Hall of Fame. He trained a long line of champion horses. It was a privilege to work with and watch a world-class trainer like Jerry. His son, Richie, was the driver.

Once my major league career started winding down, I began to think of business ventures and other things I might like to do. One of my first business ventures began the winter before I went to Japan in 1980. I saw a market for a store that sold jerseys that represented each of the teams in the Major League Baseball and the National Football League. At that time, there were no big stores selling items like this. As such, I opened Roy White Sports Stadium at Rockaway Mall in New Jersey. As I was forming this, I talked with Gene Michael and asked him to be a partner. Gene put me in touch with a friend who had a sports store in Bergen County, New Jersey. After a positive meeting, we partnered up. This was essential because I needed a partner to be able to run the operation when I was in Japan. This was a unique store. The inside was made to look like a baseball infield. We even had an Astroturf floor. In the off-season I worked the cash register and interacted with the customers, many of whom were fans. We kept this venture for a few years, but once I got into coaching, it was more difficult for me. My partner also had a different vision for the store, and when I'd come back, I'd see that he had added other items and made the store much more cluttered. His vision for the store and mine were different. When I got into coaching, I had him buy me out.

Another avenue I found myself in grew out of one of the

aspects of Japanese culture that most interested me—art. In my years in Japan, I often frequented art museums and galleries. It was a great way to spend some of the down time, especially early on when I was just learning the language and the culture. As I went to the various art houses, I quickly gained an appreciation for the uniqueness of the great art I saw. There was a gallery, named Kato, about two blocks from my apartment. That was one of the first places I went to in my spare time. I was so enamored by Japanese art that I soon began to acquire some pieces. The piece that first spoke to me, one I purchased and still have, is a wood block print of a horse. It is one of the most beautiful works of art I have ever seen.

I became so interested in art and dealing art that I opened a gallery in Ridgewood, New Jersey. I called it the Roy-San Gallery. (San was the Japanese form for "mister." In Japan, people who knew me well called me Roy-San, translated as "Mr. Roy.") For a few years, I bought and sold fine art from Japan to an appreciative clientele.

My separation from the game didn't last long, though. Within a year or so, I found myself as a coach in the Yankees system once again.

It all began with a call from Billy Connors, a minor league pitching coach at the time, who made me aware that the Yankees wanted me to be an outfield coach for the minor leagues. This was in the late 1980s. The Yankees had some tremendous young players who I was happy to work with. One such player was Bernie Williams who became a World Champion numerous times and today is a Yankees legend. When I worked with Bernie, it was clear that he possessed a great deal of talent, but it was also clear that there was a lot of work to do to harness that talent. I loved working with Bernie Williams. Like me, he was a switch hitter. He was a great student. He took my direction and advice to heart. Like so many great players, he worked tremendously hard. That diligence helped him become a star.

In those years, I also worked with Dan Pasqua, Gerald Williams, Ricky Ledee, Shane Spencer, and Jay Buhner. Each of those players also impacted the game at the major-league level as players. Also in the system at the time was an in-fielder named Buck Showalter who never reached the big leagues as a player but who, of course, became a long time and very successful major league manager with the Yankees, Diamondbacks, Rangers, Orioles, and Mets.

The Yankees must have also felt that I had an eye for talent because they also asked me, when I wasn't traveling to the various minor league affiliates, to do some scouting of amateur players who they might consider signing. I even spent some time scouting players in Japan. Two of the players I saw, Hideki Matsui and Ichiro Suzuki, would eventually star in the major leagues. I gave them high marks. I always felt that the best players in Japan would also be stars in the United States. Ichiro and Hideki proved me correct. I was told that I had a big hand in Hideki Matsui becoming a Yankee, if not directly.

Years after I sent in my report on Hideki Matsui, the Yankees' brass were having a close discussion and debate about whether or not to sign Hideki Matsui and bring him to New York. Matsui was a great player in Japan, but some in the organization weren't sure he would make the transition to major league baseball and especially the Yankees. As they were debating, one person said, "Roy White scouted him a few years back." They went back and read my report on Matsui and that made the difference. Based on my positive report, the Yankees signed Hideki Matsui. Later, he would be a key member of the 2009 World Champion Yankees. Matsui had also been a champion in Japan with the Yomiuri Giants. He and I are the only players to win championships with both the New York Yankees and the Yomiuri Giants.

Coaching for big league organizations is not a job that brings with it a lot of long-term job security. The leadership of teams changes frequently and with that comes changes in coaches and scouts and so much more. By the late 1990s, I was once again on the outside of baseball looking in. A few years later, I heard from Ray Negron who told me that the Oakland A's were looking for a minor league hitting coach. In sports, sometimes things happen quickly. In 1999, I became a coach for the Vancouver Canadians, then from 2000-03, I was the hitting coach for the Sacramento River Cats.

One of the best things that happened the year I was in Vancouver was the fact that I was able to reacquaint myself with my good friend and former minor league teammate Ian Dixon who lived in Vancouver. Just as John Sipin helped acclimate me to Japan and Japanese baseball, Ian played a big role in helping to make me and my wife comfortable in Vancouver, Canada.

Baseball also played a role in keeping my family safe on a tragic day in history. On September 10, 2001 we played our last game of the season, a playoff loss in St. Lake City. My flight home after the game brought me back after midnight. My daughter and wife drove to Kennedy Airport to pick me up. By the time we got back to our home in Toms River, it was after 2:30 am. My daughter then drove to her home in Jersey City and overslept and was not at the World Trade Center Station when the tragedy of September 11 occurred.

The teams I coached in Sacramento were loaded with talent. The great future A's pitchers, Mark Mulder, Rich Harden, and Barry Zito were all on the 2003 championship club along with future Rookie of the Year winner Bobby Crosby.

One of the nicest tributes I received regarding my years of coaching with Oakland came from Eric Hinske who won the American League Rookie of the Year Award in 2002 and whom I had coached in 2001 in Sacramento. Often coaches live in anonymity. We get recognized and remembered only when things go wrong. Eric Hinske gave me credit for teaching him how to hit to all fields when he won the Rookie of the Year Award. It was nice to receive that recognition.

In 2004 and 2005, I was back with the Yankees serving as the first base coach and working with the outfielders. Gene Michael, an old teammate from the 1970s and one of the most highly respected executives in the sport, convinced George Steinbrenner to bring me back on board. Gene Michael always respected my knowledge of the game and my ability to understand and analyze hitters. It was because of Michael that I secured my final job as a major league coach for the 2004 and

2005 seasons. In those years, the Yankees again came close, but weren't quite good enough to reach the World Series.

I was thrilled in those years to work with Hideki Matsui. We shared a common bond as we had both played with the Yomiuri Giants and the New York Yankees. We were also both left fielders. Matsui was a great student. And like Sadaharu Oh, his English was also a lot better than my Japanese.

Those 2004-05 Yankees were managed by Joe Torre who was an outstanding manager and a professional in every manner of the word. Joe trusted the coaches and let us do our jobs. He created a comfortable atmosphere to work in. There is a reason he was so successful and is now in the Hall of Fame. With those teams, the respect from the top down, from Joe through all of the coaches, was the best that it could have been. In 2004, my old teammates Willie Randolph and Mel Stottlemyre were on the coaching staff with me. My former student, Don Mattingly, as well. We all worked so well as professionals with mutual respect together. Mattingly and Stottlemyre were with me again in 2005, but Willie had left the Yankees to be the manager of the New York Mets.

During those years, the collaboration between the coaches helped lead to the Yankees' success. I wasn't the hitting coach, but when I'd see things, I'd share them with Don Mattingly who oversaw the hitters. On one occasion, I saw a flaw in Derek Jeter's batting stance and swing. I encouraged Mattingly to work with Jeter on opening up his stance. They did just that, and Jeter, who had been in a long slump, started hitting again.

Another player who I gave advice to was Alex Rodriguez. This came about naturally as we were standing by the batting cage. I saw the bat A-Rod was using and felt he would better off with a heavier model. I believe his was only 31 ounces. The next day I brought him one of my model bats, from my playing days. This was a 34 oz. model. Alex tried it in the cage, but went back to his lighter bat for the rest of the season. He eventually switched to the heavier bat and won the MVP Award. I saw A-Rod at the team's annual "Welcome Home" dinner before the season. As we passed in the hall, he thanked me for the hitting advice.

Of course, looking back, that 2004 Yankees season ended in very disappointing fashion. We were one win away from reaching the World Series, ready to knock off the Red Sox yet again, and keep the famous 86-year "Curse of the Bambino" alive when the Red Sox rallied to win four consecutive games against us as they reached, and then won, the World Series.

Making this especially hard for me was the fact that Mark Bellhorn hit a big home run against us in Game 6. A few years prior, when he and I were both in the Oakland organization, I had been Bellhorn's coach. That series loss was a true jab in the ribs. It was one of the lowest points I ever experienced in baseball. When you're a coach, and things are falling apart on the field, you are kind of helpless. The players on the team, have to do it. And that year, with those Yankees, they just couldn't turn back the momentum the Red Sox gained in that playoff series.

In 2005, the season ended even more abruptly. We lost in the first round of the playoffs to the Los Angeles Angels of Anaheim.

When one works in baseball, even with the Yankees, he's sometimes asked to do things that seem a bit ridiculous. I was always known as a player who gave it everything he had, but I was not a player who showed up umpires or argued on the field. I did my job and, for the most part, played it cool. In these years with the Yankees, I was told by the front office that I was not being demonstrative enough when bad calls were made by the umpires even though this, of course, was not my style. I was told in no uncertain terms that I had to argue with them more. I remember a game against the Mets. There was a bang-bang play at first base and our batter was out. I ran over to the umpire pretending to be mad and said, "I have to argue with you or I'm going to get fired." He let me carry on for a little bit and said, "I understand Roy." Over the next few weeks, I did this a few more times. Soon, the umpires got tired of it. Me too. It also didn't help. No call was ever overturned.

Being a coach under George Steinbrenner, your job was never 100% safe. If the team started going bad, and we had now faced two disappointing postseasons in a row, there was always the possibility that a coach or an entire staff might not return. Even in his later years, George Steinbrenner liked to shake things up. After the 2005 season, many of the coaches didn't return. This included Joe Girardi, Mel Stottlemyre, Luis Sojo, Neil Allen, and me.

For my baseball career, this was the end. I would never again serve as a coach with any franchise. I was now 61 years old and officially retired from the game.

Collaborating on the
Roy White Foundation
By Murray Bauer

Murray Bauer is the CEO of the Roy White Foundation.

***

AS FAR AS BASEBALL players go, there might not have ever been a player as classy as Roy White. That's saying a lot. I am fortunate to know many ballplayers and ex-ballplayers. Most of them have dignity and class. But none has more than Roy White.

As far as people go, there might not be any that are as classy as Roy White. That's saying a whole lot more.

I have been friends with Roy White since the 1970s, over fifty years. We do all the things that friends do. We get together for breakfast or lunch or dinner. We go places. We talk on the phone. We talk all the time. And we talk about everything— including, of course, baseball.

I have seen Roy White in so many social situations, places where he'd probably rather be left alone, but is recognized and approached by fans or celebrity hounds. He always treats the people that approach him with respect. I have never seen him turn down an autograph request. He's never been rude to a fan, even if his own dinner or social time is being interrupted. That's just who Roy White is. He's a good man. An honest man. A family man. Roy White was a great Yankee for a long time, yet he remains modest and humble. He's a great friend and a class act.

When we do charity work, Roy often is approached by

some big-time people—celebrities, CEOs, and the like. I've seen the chairman of companies become a kid again around Roy. They are in awe of his presence. I understand it. Completely. Even today, more than 40 years after he left the Yankees, fan mail for Roy White comes to my office every single day. Roy signs everything. Again, that's the kind of guy he is. He's been signing autographs for 60 years. It takes a special person to remain humble and modest in the face of such adulation, but, again, that is who Roy White is.

The Roy White Foundation was Roy's idea. We talked about how to develop something special for high school kids going off to college. Roy wanted to give back to the communities that have been so good to him—Compton, California and also Bergen County, New Jersey and of course New York. We thought long and hard about how to help college-age kids. And we wanted to do something big for them, but our foundation isn't flowing with money so the idea of big scholarships wasn't an option. That's when we hit upon the idea of books and baseball. It just seemed to fit so well. Books and Baseball. Roy is an avid reader.

I know when I went to school, I needed money for things like books. I remember first getting to college and while most of my financial matters were in order, I soon realized I needed to buy my textbooks. Seeing how expensive my textbooks were, I wondered how I'd ever be able to afford them. With our foundation, we figured that we could alleviate that concern for kids for the first year. Recipients of the Roy White Foundation Scholarships get their books paid for by us. It has worked so well. It makes Roy and all of us at the Foundation so pleased when we know that we are able to help good, young students who are in need.

Unfortunately, in recent years, due to Covid and lockdowns, the Foundation has had to take a little of a back seat. We had some big events planned including a huge concert honoring our friend Jay Black, former lead singer of Jay and the Americans. We signed contracts for major singers and their groups for a concert in Westchester County Center in White Plains, NY. We are now looking to get the Roy White

Foundation up and running again. Who knows, by the time someone is reading this, we may have already had a few events. We're working on some big ideas.

The Roy White Foundation, of course, also does other charity work. We sponsor a Christmas party for the less fortunate youth of New Jersey. We have been doing this for decades and helped with hundreds of children to celebrate the Christmas season. Roy also supports "Touching Bases," another high-quality program that allows people in wheelchairs and with other disabilities to play their own brand of baseball. And others by playing charity golf outings and more. Roy is very popular to this day. I get his fan mail and it never stops coming. People write to Roy telling him how much they admire him and look up to him, still, all these years later. This is because he's a good person and also because that classy approach was demonstrated on the ballfield for fifteen years on baseball's biggest stage.

I've been a strong advocate for Roy White for a long time and will continue to be. It is about time that he gets the respect that is due to him. I don't think he's been treated fairly by the Yankees. Here's a guy who did so much for the team not only as a 15-year player, he's been a coach, scout, outfield instructor, assistant general manager, but more importantly he has been a goodwill ambassador for over 57 years. When you consider that he came up he played with Mantle, Maris and Ford. Later on, with Munson, Guidry, Nettles, Chambliss, Randolph, Rivers and Jackson and so many other greats in Yankee history. Roy White bridged the gap between the championship teams of the 60's and 70's. He was a multiple-time All-Star and when the Yankees got good, Roy White was there at the biggest moments. The great Whitey Ford stated in his book *The few and chosen Roy White is the most underrated and underappreciated Yankee of all time. All he did was come to the ballpark for 15 straight years and did his job every day.*

People remember the great Yankees comeback in 1978. You know who was one of the biggest players on that squad? Roy White. The Yankees wouldn't have won the World Series without him—eight hits, nine runs, a key homerun in the first

inning of Game Three after returning to Yankee Stadium being down two games to none, and the Yankees never looked
back. They wouldn't have even caught the Red Sox. Roy was
on fire that second half and he also crushed it in the World
Series. Bucky Dent won the MVP for the World Series. Many
sports writers have told me that the MVP was between Roy
and Bucky.

If you look down the lists of the greatest Yankees, ever,
you'll continually find Roy White's name among the leaders
in almost every statistic. No one has played in more games in
leftfield than Roy White. He's seventh all-time in games overall as a NY Yankee. Roy is in the top-15 of all time Yankee records including hits, doubles, walks, runs scored, runs batted
in, stolen bases, fielding... on and on. He was a great defensive
player. If there was an ESPN SportsCenter when Roy White
played, he would have been on it every night. How many times
did Roy White leap over that leftfield wall to rob a player of a
home run?

Why he doesn't get the respect he deserves from the
Yankees is dumbfounding. How is it possible after his historic career spanning generations of players, that they hav-
en't made a *Yankeeography* for him. He believes the retired
uniforms are for players like Ruth, Gehrig, DiMaggio, Mantle,
Jeter, Ford and Mo. He certainly deserves a plaque. He's never
even been asked to throw out the first pitch at a postseason
game, it's just wrong.

The Yankees seem to like to highlight the players that carried on—on the field. Roy just wasn't the type to do that, to
break water coolers all the time. He didn't argue with umps
or kick dirt. He didn't make a scene. He just played baseball
the right way—what they used to call the Yankees way. Lou
Gehrig would have liked playing with Roy White. That's the
kind of player he was. It is time for the Yankees to honor this
player—a living legend, one the best Yankees ever. Roy White
has been overlooked for too long.

A final note about my friend Roy. He played the game the
right way. He hit behind runners. He bought almost a thousand walks. He was a major-league leader in sacrifice flies,

6th in Yankee history in stolen bases. He played a 162-game season every inning without making an error and that's when they played afternoon games with the infamous left field sun. He was a clutch player as solid as they come. There needs to be a place for the very few people like Roy White in baseball history.

Off the field, he's a great man too. He's a devoted husband to his amazing wife Linda. A great dad and grandfather. His children are successful. And why not? What a role model they have for a father.

Roy is such a well-rounded person. A lover of music, books, art and movies. He always makes time for others. Roy White came back as a youngster who had to fight polio as he laid in a hospital for over a year. He barely discusses that difficult start to his life.

It's an honor to call Roy White a great friend. Through the good times and the difficult times in life, I know that I can count on my brother Roy.

Chapter 16
The Former Ball Player
2005 to Today

IAM ALWAYS AMAZED, and greatly appreciate it when fans see me and tell me how important I was in their lives. I still live in New Jersey and when I'm at the store, or a restaurant, or anywhere, people come up to me and they thank me for playing hard, for being a good guy. Many call me a "true Yankee." They say I played with class. I appreciate all of that, tremendously.

What does a former ballplayer do in his retirement? What does anyone do? In our later years, things change. We can't do what we once did, but we can also, in different ways, do more.

Retirement from the game gives me time to be with my family. I have a wonderful grandson, named Henry. He is on the autistic spectrum. I am very involved in his life. I often take him to school and help him with his homework and we play together.

I also still believe in keeping in shape and I do what I can. I still play golf and I involve myself in various charity golf outings. I enjoy these, as I often get to see and play with and against my old teammates or opponents and interact with appreciative fans. We have a lot of laughs.

I am also asked to do lots of baseball card shows. Sometimes, as former players, we still have to pinch-hit. Recently, I was planning on working on this book, but I had to appear at a card show when I got a call that Joe Pepitone was unable to make it to an appearance. Just like when we were on the field, we still have each other's backs.

I also loved to attend the Yankees Fantasy Camps to see

my old teammates and the fans there as well. Some of those attendees we play against are pretty good. They always get a thrill out of getting us out or getting a big hit. The love of baseball, however we enjoy the game, never ends.

I am always honored when I am invited back to Old Timer's Day at Yankee Stadium. It's a special thrill to hear my name announced and to run out on the field, still, to the cheers from the fans. That never gets old. I missed this event so much during those first years of Covid. It was great to be back in 2022.

And yes, even today, I'm still a fan. I watch a lot of the Yankees games and will be as excited as many fans when they next win a World Championship.

People feel I have a lot to say about success, hard work, motivation, and being a great teammate and leader. For that reason, I appear at corporate events (sometimes at Yankee Stadium), Little League dinners, schools, and the like. If I can help make a positive difference in other people's lives, I am still doing my job. As ball players, we were given a special opportunity. I am glad, always, to be able to give back.

Finally, I invest time in my charity organization, the Roy White Foundation. This wonderful venture started when Vinnie Annunziatta, a friend and business partner said, "Roy, you should do a foundation." He asked me to think of a cause that I could stand for to help others. After much thought and discussion, I decided to try to help kids going to college. That's what the Roy White Foundation was founded for. We have a theme, "Books and Baseball." Through this, we help kids buy their textbooks when they head off to college. To date we have helped about 200 kids with their book expenses. Unfortunately, like so much that changed during Covid, the foundation had to take a step back in those years. We were just starting to really grow. Murray Bauer, who runs the Roy White Foundation, had arranged a huge gala event that highlighted Jay Black. This was going to be huge, but when everything was shut down, so too did the big fundraiser. We are just starting plans to get everything going again. Our first event was in the fall of 2022 at Ramapo College. It was great. Titled

"An Evening with Roy White," I had the chance to talk with the attendees about my career and so much more. It was great to be back.

Watch carefully, there might be a Roy White Foundation event coming soon to your area.

***

I have been truly blessed. As a child, I fell in love with baseball. I played the game and loved every minute. It wasn't always easy. Sometimes we strike out. Sometimes we are traded or sent to the minor leagues. Sometimes we get injured.

Sometimes we play for managers we love and other times not so much. But every person we play with, for, or against, adds something to our lives. I tried to always give something back to the others, whether that was through showing respect on the ball field, or giving my all, the game and my teammates and the fans always deserved my best. I always worked hard to give it to them. Always.

It all began in Compton. And then I made it to the Bronx. And then Japan. It all goes full circle. I had a wonderful career. I have good and loyal friends and a loving family.

It's been great. Thank you for your support. I hope to see you at a fund raiser or even at Yankee Stadium. I can't wait until the next time I am there and can hear my name over the loudspeakers again...

"And in left field, number six... ROY WHITE!"

Appendix 1
Four of the Greatest Players Ever:
Mantle, Munson, Jackson, and Oh...
What Made Them Great

I **PLAYED WITH AND** against a host of All-Stars, superstars, legends, and Hall of Famers. Over my long career as a player and coach, I had the ability to see what makes greatness, to see, clearly, those characteristics that lead to success. Among the players I played with, four stand out as players who define those characteristics absolutely.

Mickey Mantle was one of the most talented baseball players of all time. He played for 18 seasons, all with the Yankees. Mickey was a three-time Most Valuable Player and an All-Star twenty times. Mickey played in twelve World Series and was on seven World Series winning teams. Mickey was a switch hitter, like me, who clubbed 536 home runs and drove home more than 1,500 runs. He is, of course, in the Hall of Fame.

What stands out the most for me regarding Mickey Mantle is the fact that he gave his all, always. By the time I played with Mantle, he was in his final years. His body was breaking down. Before each game, day-after-day, all season long, the trainers would work with Mickey to get him able to even get out on the field. They would wrap him in athletic tape, in a way to hold him together. Mickey Mantle never looked for the easy way out. Even in his last seasons, he played almost every day. Mickey Mantle played in 144 games in each of his last two seasons. When I was Mantle's teammate, he was already a Yankees legend, yet he never rested on his laurels or his reputation. We went out and he played, hard, each game. He gave his all. I remember times early in my career when I'd be tired and wondering how I would be able to go out and play and then looked over to see Mickey Mantle getting wrapped so he could play. Seeing this example, I was determined to always play hard. If Mickey Mantle could get himself out there, I most certainly could as well.

I was the only player who was Thurman Munson's teammate for his entire career. I consider that a very special honor. Thurman Munson was one of my closest friends on the Yankees. Our lockers were right next to each other. We would talk every single day all season long. We did this for ten years. Thurman Munson was a player who defined what it is to work hard and be focused on excellence. He is not in the Baseball Hall of Fame, but he should be. Thurman Munson was among the greatest players of the 1970s, and his career would have continued if he didn't die in a terrible plan crash when he was only 32 years old. Still, in his shortened career, Thurman was the player who led the Yankees. He was a player who helped bring the franchise back to greatness. Thurman Munson's leadership was a major reason why the Yankees went to three consecutive World Series (1976-78) winning two of them. Munson was a seven-time All-Star. He won the Most Valuable Player Award in 1976. He was also the Rookie of the Year in 1970.

That Rookie of the Year Award speaks to who Thurman Munson was as a player as much as his MVP a few years later. Both awards were awarded to him because of his excellence on the field and his tremendous leadership. Thurman was a catcher, the leader on the field of play. He often batted third in the lineup, the spot, many say, where a team's most important hitter bats. When people see films of Thurman Munson, they often see him in pain overcoming hobbling on the field and yet refusing to quit. That was an aspect of Thurman's game. He was hard-nosed. He never gave an inch. Mickey Mantle had the gift of tremendous talent. Thurman Munson had to work for everything he accomplished. I never saw a player give of himself more than Thurman Munson did. In addition to being such a determined player, Thurman Munson was also a great teammate. He knew how to inspire us all; he always knew the right thing to say. I'll never forget his positive outlook in 1978 as we'd get to the ballpark each day as we were slowly, day-by-day, catching the Red Sox. He never lost hope and it was his faith in himself and the team that helped us come back from 14 games back to catch the Red Sox in the amazing season. Thurman's leadership made a difference on those teams. It's not a coincidence that after he died, the Yankees didn't win another World Series for 17 seasons.

When Reggie Jackson came to the Yankees, we had already been a World Series team having lost to the Cincinnati Reds in 1976. With Reggie came this sense of greatness. Reggie Jackson was the first superstar player, a player in some ways bigger than life, who I played with who was in his prime when he arrived. I saw Thurman Munson quickly grow into that type of player. I played with Mickey Mantle after he was already great, when Reggie arrived, as it was said, he brought his superstardom with him. Reggie had already been a seven time All-Star when he arrived in the Bronx. He had won a Most Valuable Player award. Reggie had also already been in five post seasons and was on three World Series winners with the Oakland A's. Reggie was the big star on those great A's teams. In his career, Reggie blasted 563 homers and drove home over 1,700 runs. He is also in the Baseball Hall of Fame.

People often remember the controversy regarding Reggie and Billy Martin in those first years that he was a Yankee. There were newspaper reports almost daily. Reggie and Billy were never at a loss for words, and many of them weren't complimentary toward the other. There was a reason Graig Nettles referred to those years as a circus and why Sparky Lyle called those years the Bronx Zoo. What people also remember was that famous game in 1977 when Billy Martin pulled Reggie Jackson from a game in Fenway Park in the middle of an inning because he felt Reggie wasn't hustling. Reggie wasn't dogging it on that play. I was in left field. I saw it all. Reggie misplayed the ball, but he certainly was not loafing. Reggie didn't loaf. Reggie talked a lot before the games, and after the games, but once he was on the field, he played hard. Reggie wanted to win. It's not a coincidence that when Reggie Jackson went to a team, that team won. Reggie also had an attribute that many players do not have, even the great ones. Mickey Mantle had this trait as well (no one has hit more home runs in the World Series that Mickey Mantle), as did Thurman Munson (who hit .357 in the post season over his career), but no could rise to the occasion like Reggie did. We'd often note that if it was a nationally televised game, that Reggie would probably come through and hit a home run. And he did more often than not. No one will ever forget how he hit three homers on three swings off three different pitchers in the game that clinched the 1977 World Series for us. Great players can find something deep inside them, another level, if you will, when the team needs them most. Reggie could do this—and he did, often. Great players don't let the moments intimidate them; they find a way to be bigger than the moment. That come from confidence in one's ability. It also comes from the hard work they put in beforehand knowing that they are ready. Confidence, preparation, and determination are characteristics that Reggie Jackson had. He gave his all. That's why he was a winner.

No player in the Major Leagues has ever his 800 home runs in his career. And no player in Japan has as well, except for one man, the great Sadaharu Oh. In his career, Oh blasted an amazing 868 home runs. He drove home more than 2,000 runs. I have often said that this wasn't just because he played in Japan. As Ichiro Suzuki, Hideki Matsui, and others have shown, the greatest Japanese players can also perform at star levels, even Hall of Fame levels, in the United States. If he had played in America, Sadaharu Oh would have been a superstar. He was that good. Proof of his greatest comes with the number nine. Oh was the Most Valuable Player in nine different seasons. His teams also once won nine consecutive Japan Series (the equivalent of the World Series in the USA). Sadaharu Oh was a superstar, a rare talent, the best of the best, for a long, long time.

Like the others in this essay, Sadaharu Oh was a player who worked tremendously hard at his craft. In Japan hard work in training is a requisite, but Oh worked harder than most. His focus, which originally came from samurai training, defined his approach to the game. Oh used the attributes of zen to be able to stay in the moment. Other players, in Japan and America, would lose their focus. In fact, most players do from time to time. The great players are able to focus more than others, but no player focused as well as Sadaharu Oh. He was always in the moment. He was always prepared. He knew that his preparation was greater than that of his opponent and this led to much of his success.

As I look back that these four great players, I see many of the same winning characteristics. I see players who gave their all. I see players who were able to rise to the occasion, to make themselves bigger than the moment. I see players who understood that hard work and preparation are the keys to success. But what I also didn't mention, was that each of these players faced hardships as well.

When Mickey Mantle first arrived in the big leagues, he did so poorly that he was on the verge of quitting. At the end of his career, in 1966, Mickey played in just 108 games. People wondered if he could be an everyday player ever again.

Thurman Munson had initial success as a rookie, but then saw his production decline. After hitting over .300 as a rookie, he hit just .251 the next year. And we all know that in the early years of his career, the Yankees just didn't win often enough.

When Reggie Jackson came to New York, he struggled. Reggie didn't hit much, he had a poor relationship with his manager and many of his teammates, and even asked to be traded. In his first season in New York, it looked as though Reggie Jackson's Yankees tenure would be a failure.

In Sadaharu Oh's first professional season, he didn't even hit .200. He was a huge disappointment to his team and himself. He didn't have a .300 batting average until his fifth season. He would then hit .300 or better for eight years in a row.

Like everyone, success didn't just come to these players, or even stay with these players. They continually had to work at their craft, they had to always stay focused, and they had to maintain the focus that is necessary to be successful and to be a winner.

Each of these players didn't let failure define them. They found ways to modify their game to become successful. Each of these players were such leaders and winners that they made their teammates better, so much so that they were all champions multiple times. Because of all of this, each of these players were winners.

What makes a winner? I think the answer can be found in the word itself:

W – Winners <u>Work</u> hard

I – Winners <u>Invest</u> in themselves and their teammates

N – Winners <u>Never Quit</u>

N – Winners are <u>Not Satisfied</u> with being just good enough—they seek to be their best, always

E – Winners are <u>Enthusiastic</u>

S – Winners find ways to <u>Succeed</u>

I learned a great deal from each of these legendary players and was honored to spend parts of my career playing alongside and learning from each of them.

Appendix 2
What Made Roy White Successful
By Paul Semendinger

ROY WHITE HAD A tremendous baseball career. He played for the Yankees and Tokyo Giants and won championships in America and Japan. He also played with and against some of the best players to ever play the game. He is remembered and honored as one of the best players ever to play for the New York Yankees—arguably their best left fielder of all time.

When I have been out with Roy White, people, often middle-aged men, come up to him and tell him what a difference he made in their lives. They approach him respectfully and ask to shake his hand or take a picture with him. They often relate what an honor it is to meet him. Almost always they thank him for what he did. Sometimes I sit back and reflect on all of this. What did Roy White do? He played baseball. But he played baseball in a way that made him memorable.

Roy White played ball in a way many others didn't. I think this is what the fans saw in him. They saw a player who gave of himself every single game. He never let up. He always worked to do his best. Roy White knew he owed that to his team and himself. And, in a way, he knew he owed it to the fans who came and supported him. New York is a demanding place to play baseball (Tokyo too!). The fans ask a lot of the players. They want greatness. They expect championships. But they also want more. They want and expect each player to maximize his talents to be the best player he can be. I believe that is why Roy White was able to be a Yankee for so long, why the fans cheered him, and why they still come up to him, just to say thanks. Throughout his career, he tried to exemplify what it is to be a Yankee—a player who gave his best always and who became a winner.

I believe there are a few attributes about Roy White's

approach to baseball, and life, that allowed him to be successful. I learned a great deal from him as we wrote this book together. It is my hope that in sharing these big ideas here, that others can learn from Roy White's example and can find ways to maximize their own skills and talents.

We cannot let our circumstances define us:

Roy White came from very humble beginnings. His parents were an interracial couple in a time when that was not accepted. It was a big reason why their marriage did not work out. He lived in poverty in a dangerous inner city. He was very sick as a child and had a disease (polio) that often led to a debilitating condition that led to lifetime disabilities. But never once did he allow any of those factors to define himself. Roy White never looked at his circumstances and asked others to feel sorry for him. He knew that if he was going to become successful, that he would have to be the person who made that happen. Roy White knew that he was in control of his life. He understood that he needed to be a good student and that if he was going to be a ball player, that it was going to take a tremendous amount of hard work. He also always had a positive "can-do" attitude. He knew he didn't have to accept the circumstances that surrounded his childhood—that he could be more than that. If he didn't become a ballplayer, he would have gone to college. There were many avenues that he could have taken to find success. I am certain of this. If Roy White hadn't been a baseball player, he would have been successful in whatever career he chose.

Success breeds success:

Roy White was very fortunate in that the area where he grew up was what one might call a "hotbed" of baseball talent. A host of the kids he played baseball with on the sandlots, in Little League, and in organized ball (American Legion and high school) went on to become professionals. Many would become all-stars. Each of these players set their own examples for Roy White to follow. He could see how talented they were and what they did to become better at their craft. As the players a few years older than him were signed to professional contracts, he quickly learned what it would take to follow their paths into professional baseball.

Working hard matters:
Hard work matters. Not all of the talented kids Roy White played with earned contracts. Not all of the guys who went professional made it to the big leagues. And not all became all-stars or world champions. Roy White saw what those who became successful did—in short, they worked hard. Great players don't just rely on their natural talent, they work diligently to hone that talent. They seek advice from others: teammates or coaches. They observe what others do to become better. They invest in the task at hand and give their all to be the best they can be. The players who didn't work as hard, were most often the ones who didn't make it. Many of those players had more natural ability than others; they just didn't have the focus and determination, or they just didn't work hard enough to maximize the talents they had.

We cannot let others define us:
Early on in Roy White's baseball career, he had to play baseball as a black man in the Jim Crow south, an area defined by racism and segregation. The society he lived in during the summers that he played baseball told him (in words and actions) that he was not equal to others; that he was inferior because of his race. At baseball games on the road, especially, the fans would yell racial epitaphs at him. They let him know how little they thought of him as a human being. It is difficult to explain what a challenge it must have been to face that every day, for years, as he worked his way through the minor leagues. Yet, he did. He was able to persevere because he knew that he wasn't the person that society and those fans said he was. Roy White knew that he had value. He would not let others define who he was. Roy White used the negativity hurled at him as a way to gather strength to do whatever it took to achieve and live out my dream as a baseball player. All these years later, Roy White is not angry at the situations he

faced. He is bigger than that. He is humble. Whenever we'd discuss this, rather than focusing on himself, he'd point out that others, the players who preceded him, had it tougher.

Being a great teammate is important:
From his earliest days on a baseball field, right up through the years he coached, Roy White saw clearly how important it is to be a good teammate. Good teammates help others. Good teammates don't look at their own statistics; rather they do whatever the team needs them to do. Good teammates find ways to be kind to all, they make the clubhouse a place where others can feel comfortable. Great teammates know and live the old adage, "there is no I in team."

Successful people learn to adapt:
Throughout his career, Roy White had to make many changes. He went from being an infielder to an outfielder—not an easy change, at all. In this, he had to learn how to play the vast expanse that was left field at Yankee Stadium and how to adapt to the unrelenting sun during day games. As a hitter, he had to learn how to adapt to better and better pitching as he worked his way up through the minor leagues. Roy also had to learn and remember what his strengths were as a hitter. At one point, he became convinced that he was a power hitter and that led him into some bad habits. He had to teach himself to use his natural swing and talents to be the best player he could be. This required him to continually adapt throughout his playing days. As Roy White aged, he also had to find new and better ways to stay in shape to stay at the top of his game. He took up karate for a few years to become more flexible and to get in the best shape he could over the winter. This helped him tremendously during spring training and in the following seasons. Roy White's off-season conditioning allowed him to be a better ballplayer. (It also helped him survive the most difficult spring training he ever had under Bill Virdon.)

Luck and chance play a role:
While we always have to do our best, luck and chance

often play big roles in our success or failure. If Joe Pepitone didn't break his arm, Roy White might never had had a chance to become a starting player. I also think about Rich Beck, drafted into the military one day before he was ineligible for the draft. Beck had a promising career that was cut short as a result. Sometimes we just need to be in the right place at the right time.

Winners stay positive:

If we look around us, there are plenty of things to get us down. On a baseball team, and in life, if we focus on the bad, we will tend to become less motivated, less enthusiastic, and less successful. Roy White was able to play on championship teams because he, as well as many of my teammates, stayed focused on what they could do. In 1978 when everyone in baseball thought the Yankees were done as a team, Roy White and many others stayed positive. Thurman Munson and Roy would arrive at the ballpark and note how quickly they were catching the Red Sox. This inspired the team and it helped them close the gap and catch the Red Sox. Team. The players stayed positive, they believed in themselves and good things, as a result, happened.

Respect and kindness matter:

When people remember the 1977-78 Yankees, they often recall the bigger-than-life characters who contributed to making the situations around the team seem like a zoo or a circus. There seemed to be controversy everywhere. That simply wasn't true. While there were huge personalities on the team and in the organization, there were a host of players, guys like Willie Randolph, Chris Chambliss, Ron Guidry, and Roy White, who did not get mired in the negativity and who brought, as many say, a certain "class" to the team. These players formed the glue of those Yankees teams, they treated each other, and everyone, with respect. They treated the game with respect. They treated everyone, writers, broadcasters, fans... everyone, with respect. This, I feel, mattered more than people realize. Roy White and these other players helped make sure that there was a certain Yankee professionalism, even when it was overshadowed by the negativity reported in the press. This was one reason why the Yankees were able to overcome all of that negativity and still win. When he went to Japan, Roy White never assumed he was better than those players. He worked diligently to assimilate to the Japanese culture and the Japanese norms. Roy White respected the country he was in. When we give respect and kindness, it matters a great deal. It matters always. It can be the difference between success and failure.

These attributes are what define the career of Roy White. These tried-and-true actions, behaviors, and mindsets allow for success. In life there is always a certain amount of luck, but when we stay positive, when we work hard, when we do all we can to be our best, as Roy White did, always, we put ourselves in the best position to be successful in whatever we do.

Roy White led by example. He still does. Roy White is a winner. He inspires me daily.

Appendix 3
Roy White's Place Among the All-Time Yankees*

WAR (Position Players)	Games Played	At Bats
46.8 (11th)	1,881 (7th)	6,650 (9th)
Runs Scored	Hits	Walks
964 (13th)	1,803 (11th)	934 (8th)
Stolen Bases	Times on Base	Sacrifice Flies
233 (6th)	2,766 (8th)	69 (2nd)
Home Runs	Runs Batted In	Total Bases
160 (28th)	758 (20th)	2,685 (14th)

*all statistics from baseball-reference.com

Appendix 4
Roy White Compared to Select Hall of Fame Left Fielders*

	WAR	WAR7	JAWS
Roy White	46.8	37.0	41.9
Jim Rice	47.7	36.4	42.1
Lou Brock	45.3	32.0	38.6
Heinie Manush	48.0	35.9	41.9
Chick Hafey	31.2	28.1	29.6

*all statistics from baseball-reference.com

Appendix 5
Roy White's All-Time Yankees Teammate Team
(Minimum of four years played with Roy White)

C – Thurman Munson
1B – Chris Chambliss / Joe Pepitone
2B – Willie Randolph / Horace Clarke
SS – Bucky Dent / Gene Michael
3B – Graig Nettles
LF –
CF – Mickey Rivers
RF – Bobby Murcer / Lou Piniella
DH – Reggie Jackson
SP – Ron Guidry, Mel Stottlemyre, Ed Figueroa, Catfish Hunter, Fritz Peterson
RP – Sparky Lyle, Goose Gossage, Lindy McDaniel, Dick Tidrow, Jack Aker

Special Note – At the start of my career, I played with many great Yankees, but I didn't have the good fortune to play with them for a long time nor see them at their best. This includes Mickey Mantle, Elston Howard, Tom Tresh, Roger Maris, Bobby Richarsdon, and Clete Boyer, among others.

Appendix 6
Roy White's All- Opponent Team

C – Carlton Fisk
1B – Boog Powell / Harmon Killebrew
2B – Rod Carew
SS – Bert Campaneris
3B – Brooks Robinson / George Brett
LF – Carl Yastrzemski
CF – Paul Blair
RF – Tony Oliva / Frank Robinson
SP – Mike Cuellar, Luis Tiant, Jim Palmer, Bert Blyleven, Nolan Ryan, Denny McLain
RP – Rollie Fingers, John Hiller

Best Hitter – Tony Oliva. There was no pitch that could get him out. He hit the ball everywhere. He'd be the guy I wouldn't want to see with the game on the line and a runner on second. He knew how to make adjustments.

Toughest Right-Handed Pitcher – Bert Blyleven. His curve ball was just so awesome. No one had a pitch like that, fast and sharp. He also had a good fastball.

Toughest Left-Handed Pitcher – Mike Cuellar. His screwball was thrown at three different speeds: Slow, slower, and slowest. It was very difficult to time his pitches. And when you did have it timed, that's when he'd throw his fastball.

Appendix 7
Roy White's Top Five Favorite Topps Baseball Cards

#1 1974

#2 1972

#3 1978

#4 1970

#5 1971

All cards are courtesy of The Topps Company

About the Authors

Roy White:

One of the most beloved Yankees of All-Time, Roy White was an all-star outfielder for the Yankees from 1965 to 1979. Roy played in the 1977 and 1978 World Championship Yankees teams. He later played for the Tokyo Giants in Japan, coached with the Yankees, and founded the Roy White Foundation, which provides financial assistance to young adults and children whose desire to further their education is inhibited by financial complications. Roy White sits among the all-time leaders on most of the all-time Yankees lists.

Paul Semendinger:

After a wonderful 32-year career in education, Dr. Paul Semendinger is now a full-time author and part time college professor and is widely known for his knowledge of the history of baseball, specifically the New York Yankees. He is a member of the Internet Baseball Writers Association of America (IBWAA) and is the Editor-in-Chief of the successful Yankees blog, Start Spreading the News. His book *The Least Among Them*, about 29 Yankees players who only played a single game in the major leagues, as a NY Yankee, has won multiple awards. Paul lives in New Jersey with his wife.